SUE McCORD
University of Colorado, Boulder

The Storybook Journey

Pathways to Literacy
Through Story and Play

Merrill,
an imprint of Prentice Hall
Englewood Cliffs, New Jersey   Columbus, Ohio

Library of Congress Cataloging-in-Publication Data

McCord, Sue.
    The storybook journey: pathways to literacy through story and play / Sue McCord.
        p.   cm.
    Includes bibliographical references and index.
    ISBN 0-13-183997-7
    1. Literature—Study and teaching (Early childhood) I. Title.
LB1139.5L58M33   1995
372.64—dc20

95–1304
CIP

Cover art: ©Darcie Park, Red Hot Studios, 1994
Editor: Linda James Scharp
Production Editor: Julie Anderson Tober
Text Designer: Anne Flanagan
Cover Designer: Brian Deep
Production Buyer: Pamela D. Bennett
Electronic Text Management: Marilyn Wilson Phelps, Matthew Williams, Jane Lopez, Karen L. Bretz
Illustrations: Rod Hitchcock

This book was set in Century Schoolbook by Prentice Hall and was printed and bound by R.R. Donnelley and Sons Company. The cover was printed by Phoenix Color Corp.

© 1995 by Prentice-Hall, Inc.
A Simon & Schuster Company
Englewood Cliffs, New Jersey 07632

Photos by Sue McCord, except page 153, by Julie Tober

Printed in the United States of America

10 9 8 7 6 5 4 3 2 1

ISBN: 0-13-183997-7

Prentice-Hall International (UK) Limited, *London*
Prentice-Hall of Australia Pty. Limited, *Sydney*
Prentice-Hall of Canada, Inc., *Toronto*
Prentice-Hall Hispanoamericana, S. A., *Mexico*
Prentice-Hall of India Private Limited, *New Delhi*
Prentice-Hall of Japan, Inc., *Tokyo*
Simon & Schuster Asia Pte. Ltd., *Singapore*
Editora Prentice-Hall do Brasil, Ltda., *Rio de Janeiro*

TO NANA. . . .

*For her lap, her love, her spirit
and to my precious family
for being just that*

NOTES ON AN UNHURRIED JOURNEY

When we adults think of children, there is a simple truth which we ignore; childhood is not preparation for life; childhood is life.

A child isn't getting ready to live; a child is living. The child is constantly confronted with the nagging question: "What are you going to be?" Courageous would be the youngster who, looking the adult squarely in the face, would say, "I'm not going to be anything; I already am." We adults would be shocked by such an insolent remark, for we have forgotten, if indeed we ever knew, that a child is an active, participating, and contributing member of society from the time he is born.

Childhood isn't a time when he moulded into a human who will then live life; he is a human who *is* living life. No child will miss the zest and joy of living unless these are denied him by adults who have convinced themselves that childhood is a period of preparation.

How much heartache we would save ourselves if we would recognize the child as a partner with adults in the process of living, rather than always viewing him as an apprentice. How much we would teach each other . . . Adults with the experience and children with the freshness; how full both our lives could be. A little child may not lead us, but at least we ought to discuss the trip with him; for, after all, life is his journey too.

~Professor T. Ripaldi

Preface

O *ur most dependable guides to children's real needs are our own feelings about them and with them and for them. We have to accept our own childhood and use it to understand childhood feelings. Growing up is often, after all, a continuum in which older people help younger ones and those farther along reach back and help others. If we can accept our own places in the continuum, and are in touch with our own childhood feelings, we will be ready and able to help children as they struggle with the arduous and gratifying tasks of growing up.*

~Rita Warren (1977)

R eflecting on the experiences and related feelings of our own childhood is critical to our growth as human beings and as effective family members, teachers, parents, therapists, caregivers, and friends! For those of us who provide child care and education for young children, it is particularly relevant to explore some of the intense feelings of our own childhood experience, to remember how we perceived the significant times and people in our early life, and to grow in our own understandings through these personal memories. How we feel about children and how we choose to share our lives with them depend a great deal on our own childhood.

My life was deeply touched by my paternal grandmother, affectionately known as Nana. When I was four, we moved into Nana's home and I became her roommate; she was my soul mate. It seems only fair that I share a few vignettes of these early years as they have much to do with this journey.

Nana and I were two generations apart in age, but delightfully connected in family and spirit. We could share our special thoughts and dreams, giggle with and at each other, and weep openly together in our pain. Nana fostered my sense of wonder by the way she spun her lively tales of the past, including treasured glimpses into my father's childhood. She had a little tattered box she loved to bring out once in awhile that held my father's first pair of shoes, leather glove, and a curl of hair from his very first haircut. The tissue paper that held each relic smelled musty and if I close my eyes now I can still hear it rustle as I waited with anticipation. She carefully handed me the treasures and with each one there would be a wonderful memory shared. Studying her face and her deep brown eyes I would scrunch between her and the arm of the chair . . . removed to another world through her experiences.

There was a special way that Nana let me share her world. We built memories together that have sustained me forever and I believe formed the foundation for my life's work with young children. She played marches on the piano while I paraded around the living room hammering a wooden spoon against the bottom of a waste-basket. She taught me the song: "Oh What a Beautiful Morning" and my first two jokes. She patiently helped me struggle with two knitting needles and a ball of yarn as I tried to imitate her knitting. She was the only one who ever let me win in "Go Fish" and was forever my refuge in a storm. She talked with me about the pictures I drew and placed them in the drawer next to that tattered box. In the evening, I would go to bed first and reluctantly fall asleep before Nana came upstairs. One lucky night, however, I remember I was able to fake a little shut-eye long enough to take in Nana's nightly rituals. There was the application of Pond's cream gently patted on each cheek and over her nose then wiped away with a tissue; the filing and buffing of her nails; a funny kind of eye exercise she did with moving her index finger closer and further away from each eye . . . *but* it was her culminating activity that night that caught *my* eye! Nana slowly opened her top dresser drawer—off limits to me—and took out a little velvet bag with a draw string. She placed her wedding band, engagement ring, and a few other pieces of jewelry carefully inside this bag. The bag was then tied to her nighty strap. My whisper of: "Nana," broke the silence. "Why do you tie that velvet bag to your nighty strap?"

"Oh, you're still awake!" A long pause followed, then that glorious twinkle in her eyes. "Well, honey, I've decided if anyone tries to steal my treasures, they'll have to take *me* with them."

I rolled over with a "good night, Nana" and fell fast asleep with thoughts of who would ever try to steal anything from us, and maybe I should worry about that. It was not too long after that watchful night when Nana came upstairs as usual to hug me before I crawled into bed. "Oh my land, child! What have you got under your pajama top?" I quickly unpinned my knotted handkerchief from my under-shirt and proudly revealed what lay hidden inside: a smooth white rock I had found at the beach that summer, my jacks and ball set, my doll's baby shoes, and the nut my father had carved into a squirrel for me! "If anyone tries to steal my treasures, Nana, they'll have to take *me* with them too!" Nana never laughed out loud, but out of concern that I might develop a concave chest, she convinced me to pin my treasures to the pillow case.

There was time to dream and share, wish and imagine, create and experience at a pace that was not interrupted by gymnastics, ballet, or piano lessons before I really was ready to make that commitment.

If I could be endowed today with fairy tale magic, I would wish that every child on this earth could have a "Nana": at least one human being in their life who respected, understood, and loved them enough to nurture their growth, encourage their interests, know their dreams and fears, and cherish their existence. Ours is a very busy culture now. The configuration of the family is ever changing and the quiet reflective times in one's home life are rare. The extended family is often spread far across the country. Young children are more and more in the care of people outside the home and often in groups who need more trained adults. My deep concern is one of human contact and the availability of enough significant others with loving arms, laps and unhurried moments for listening . . . listening and really hearing the feelings behind a child's words or the silent communication and understanding that comes from spending meaningful time with another human being.

This may seem a long way off from storybooks, literacy, and learning, but it has everything to do with it! To become human beings, children need to grow up with other human beings who help them to believe in themselves. It may be a parent, grandparent, neighbor, teacher, or therapist who will support, share, value, nurture, respect, and confirm the importance of their existence. The emotional stability nurtured by this caring allows children the freedom and energy they rightly deserve to be able to concentrate, engage, learn, follow through and enjoy the world that is out there for them to explore.

ACKNOWLEDGMENTS

What would a journey be like without wonderful friends, colleagues, children and their families? So many people have made this adventure possible! It's with heartfelt gratitude that I thank all of those who gave me advice, support, and encouragement to write this book . . . it's been an amazing journey to completion.

To my Mapletree colleagues—Mary Culkin, Judi Morosok, and Janice Zelazo: All three were an integral part of the journey beginnings.

To Bruce and Marillyn Atchison, Dennis Mulcare, and Lu Reuter—my good friends, colleagues, and unique creators of the most wonderful journeys—I am eternally grateful for the beginning days of writing when we gathered in my living room to talk about the essence of the journey.

To Cathy Fletcher: for all of your delightful, playful O.T. extensions of the storybook journey and for giving such helpful feedback on the first draft of Part I.

To Susan Moore: for nudging me to keep going deeper and making the rich connections between the journey process and communication.

To the C.U. Boulder Crew of teachers: Marillyn Atchison, Sheila Goetz, Barb Roscoe, Janine Randol, and Eileen Conroy for the journeys, the feedback, the sharing, and the inspiration.

To Tikki Heublein, Dee Kotaska, Anita Kruger: for all of the suggestions and hard work in setting up the Minnesota seminars.

To Tracy Kovach: who ran with the journey concept and linked it to augmentative communication for the youngsters at The Children's Hospital in Denver and around the country.

To Wheelock College: for teaching me to see the whole child within the context of the family.

To Tom Lickona: a mentor, respected colleague, and masterful teacher.

To Rachel Gubman: former student, fine teacher, and honest critic.

To Joan Martin: a dear friend and inspirational colleague.

To Sue Lubeck and "the Bookies": my fondest cheerleader and favorite book consultant. She has waited a long time to hold this book in her hands!

To Suzanne Barchers: for her support and editing expertise.

To Ann Davis and Linda Scharp at Prentice Hall: for believing that this book will be a helpful resource for those working with young children. Thank you for your guidance and support.

To Julie Tober and Megan Rowe at Prentice Hall: the journey with you has been a gift.

To Brenda Dowell: a heartfelt thanks for all those early Saturday morning typing sessions and the patience to read all of my notes scribbled in every margin on every page!

To my wonderfully accepting husband, Charlie: for his loving care, patience, and endless support—not only during this voyage, but for our life's journey of 35 years.

To Jennifer and Chip, who were my greatest inspiration as a mother and a teacher. I cherish the memories of our nightly ritual of sharing all those books, stories, songs, and dramatic replays in that wonderful old farmhouse in Ithaca.

To all the families and children at the Early Childhood Language Center (ECLC), Mapletree Day Treatment Center, the Child Language Center (CLC), Boulder Day Nursery, Children's House, Make a Mess and Make Believe Child Care Center, Friends and Fun Children's Center, Northglenn Preschool, Boulder County Head Start, the United States Air Force Academy Child Care Center, Boulder County Child Care Homes, Aurora 7 Kindergarten, The Children's Hospital, and all the other centers and classrooms with teachers who came to the workshops and seminars and took the storybook journey through forests, over bridges, and into the land of Oz.

Special note: As the final words were being written on the journey, our daughter and son-in-law adopted a little two-year-old girl, Cassie. Cassie: Thank you for coming into our lives. It thrills me that you *love* books!

~Sue McCord

Brief Contents

Contents

II *Implementing the Journey*   *47*

Introduction by Invitation

To all educators who work with young children, including teachers, parents, grandparents, caregivers, paraprofessionals, speech pathologists, occupational therapists, counselors, students in training, and others who would like to travel through storybooks with children and colleagues.

You are invited to travel through this book on a journey that involves you in an exploration of possibilities. It will look at the important relationship between play and child development; the use of stories to foster genuine human relationships, and the creation of meaningful environments, curriculum, and materials derived from the themes and concepts presented in storybooks. The journey emphasizes the significance and delight of using storybooks as a means of entering the child's world. The intention is to give you enough content and inspiration that your own creativity and enjoyment of the storybook journey process will carry you, children, and their families to new avenues of learning. Some travelers want very specific maps for their journeys, while others prefer to venture into new territory, finding their own alternative routes. The storybook journey provides direction and incentive to tap your own ideas, experiences, expertise, and resources as well as to ignite a refreshing approach to your work unencumbered by a preset curriculum. The journey develops a framework to use a whole-language, literature-based learning approach as a means to integrate learning and emerging literacy into all facets of the classroom through immersion in storybooks. This is accomplished through observing the children's play and developing the program to support their interests, ideas, and creative extensions of stories.

The journey is not a method but a philosophy. It is a philosophy that is based on a solid understanding of how children develop and with a keen interest in inspiring practices that support and enhance the growth of each individual child within the context of the group. It is a philosophy that states: If stories derive personal meaning, learning from them will have a significant impact. The key element is working closely with families as well as with the children to make storybooks and storytelling an integral part of every child's life.

The storybook journey is neither a unit plan detached from the lives of children nor a series of recipes developed by adults. It is a means of inviting children to participate, read, create, draw, write, speak, communicate, listen, think, and enjoy. Through our careful observations, children will reveal to us the vital feedback necessary to assess what they are doing with stories through their play and work and how they are building and extending foundations for literacy and life learning.

Our journey with young children, as in any journey we embark on, is enhanced by dream time and thoughtful preparation. I have prepared a backpack with the essentials for my passage with young children, their families, and colleagues. It is filled with the many beliefs I carry with me as a critical sustenance for the continuous growth of this project. They are beliefs that have come from years of working with young children, dedicated teachers, and caring parents. They are *my* beliefs. You may not agree with what I carry in my pack; I just want you to know the contents before we set off together. There is also an empty backpack for you to use. If you choose, fill it with those things that are essential for *your* travels with children. It will help to guide your journey in a very personal direction.

The journey is as much about people in search of a special kind of learning and teaching as it is about storybooks and literacy. Where this journey will take all of us depends upon our past experiences, who we bumped into along the way, how much time we have given ourselves to assimilate the surroundings and how open we are to taking risks. Let's go!

This book is set up in two parts. The first part covers the philosophical background and the second part develops all phases of implementing the journey. The reader can either go from cover to cover or can readily choose specific areas of concentration, such as: setting up environments around a story theme, using and extending materials, planning a journey. Of course, I hope you will invest in reading the book all the way through to truly gather the information. However you choose to journey, enjoy your trip and remember your backpack! Then again, if your backpack is full of "old baggage," leave it behind.

STORYBOOK JOURNEY BACKPACK

Belief: that paramount to understanding the behavior and development of children is our ability to be skillful observers and recorders. Children speak to us through their behavior.

Belief: that play is the child's vehicle to understanding the world; it offers a window to the trained observer for understanding each child's unique developmental process.

Belief: that the child and the family must be the central focus in developing any program that values and initiates lifelong learning. We are in their lives for one year; parents are there forever.

Belief: that children learn best when they are allowed to pursue a personal route to knowing with support from invested adults. This is what builds competence and self-worth.

Belief: that inclusion of all children and their families into well-staffed classrooms is imperative to everyone's growth as a human being. The emphasis in such settings must be on the development of meaningful human interactions.

Belief: that future training should prepare all staff in all settings to work with all children regardless of their diverse cultural heritage, learning style, or developmental abilities. It is a challenge to be met in partnership with parents.

Belief: that the learning should be the dynamic interaction and integration of humans, environment, and materials.

Belief: that adults working with young children need to be supported in their efforts to sustain their own learning and encouraged to stay abreast of their own needs.

Belief: that being in touch with our own childhood is important. The personal pursuit of knowing what it was like for each of us as a child and how that might affect our lives with children today, is a powerful way to increase our understanding of and effective work with young children.

PERSONAL BELIEF BACKPACK

The Storybook Journey

Pathways to Literacy
Through Story and Play

Philosophical Underpinnings

*I*t's nice to have an end to journey
towards, but it's the journey that matters
in the end.

~Ursula K. LeGuin

The Storybook Journey

The Evolution of a Process

This chapter will

- *Discuss the power and meaning of stories*
- *Give an overview of the journey process, procedures, and possibilities*
- *Discuss the story selection process*
- *Ponder what makes the storybook journey unique*

PROLOGUE

The magnetism of stories in the lives of children is significant. They listen to them with more than their ears; they absorb them through their souls, and through a closeness and shared enjoyment with other human beings. The very young snuggle up close, making the significant other's lap one of the first and warmest literacy environments. They listen with an ever-expanding notion of what is possible through entering and sharing the world of storybook characters.

Stories provide windows and reference points. They translate an experience into understanding through another form and at a safe distance as well as offer options and alternatives for looking at some of life's more complicated issues. Is it any wonder, then, that youngsters can identify with Humpty Dumpty and those "falling apart" experiences we have all had when it's hard to pull ourselves back together or to fix a broken toy? There is a novelty in watching this whimsical, egg-shaped character dramatize so vividly that all does not always go as planned and that sometimes not even powerful king's horses or king's men can fix everything. Humpty, in his own simple way, serves as that meaningful reference point or window for a look at life's rougher moments. We are also aware that for the very young, Humpty fulfills their need merely to imitate the joy and surprise of falling off of anything resembling a wall—and, if luck will have it, maybe bumping into a friend on the way down.

Stories—whether told through nursery rhymes, songs, imagination, or storybooks—can provide a very meaningful avenue to children who are searching to orient themselves in the world. All of us know the power stories have had in our lives and the significance of our own life's story. For all of us, our experiences become the unique material for our personal narrative. As adults we can paint, sculpt, write, or otherwise communicate our memories and reflections in various forms. Children are only beginning to gather their experiences and personal stories. Their means of sharing the impact are usually limited to the here and now. Storybooks thus become a way of relating their lives to the lives of the characters and a means of matching some of their feelings with the characters' experiences. Stories do not intend to give answers, but allow children to extrapolate meanings that are relevant to them. You might be having a troll-like day and just want people out of your way or perhaps identifying with Max in *Where the Wild Things Are*. Maurice Sendak has the magic ability to remember what it is like to be a child. He gets right inside children's thoughts and in a special way elaborates their fantasies. All of us know how this story touches them as they want to hear it over and over again. It reveals a world where controls are hard and warm dinners awaiting bruised prides are wonderful. For many children, though, this may be a rare outcome and the fantasy of the story their only relief. Every aspect of human development has the potential to become an integral part of the child's love affair with this precious medium. The storybook journey provides one approach among many for the child and the adult to learn about each other, the world, and oneself.

JOURNEY OVERVIEW

The journey you are on offers an opportunity to travel through the joys and challenges of living and learning with young children. It is a dynamic, evolving process, one that uses children's literature and spontaneous play as the main vehicle for the pilgrimage. Fueling the journey is the children's insatiable desire to learn, their sheer delight in sharing the total story experience, and the story's appeal and predictable familiarity. The storybook journey planning and the children's play become the instruments to elaborate their experiences and life events. The children are immersed in literature, but always in conjunction with all of the other available program and environmental alternatives, as well as the children's personal engagement with their own pursuits.

The young child in today's world is influenced by the many pressures of a high-tech, fast-paced, automated, ever-changing society. Television, being one of the most dominant and influential factors in the child's mechanical world, can be viewed as a prime inhibitor of the child's imaginative play and a substitute for interactive story reading/telling, dramatic play, and social feedback. Stories being read or told by a warm, interactive human being provide a refreshing alternative to the electronic media's hype of the superheroes with their plotless ramblings and confusing messages.

Threads that exist in children's own lives weave in and out of each story. That familiarity appears to motivate, ignite, and replenish their ability to take part in and derive personal meaning from the story. It creates a way for children to become connected to the special people in their lives.

CREATING THE PROCESS

The journey essentially builds on the themes and concepts in a story to spin a learning web of ideas and experiences. Story themes are then integrated with areas of the curriculum to support the child's physical, social, emotional, and cognitive development.

This is best accomplished when the adults

- are philosophically cohesive and can work collaboratively as a team
- understand what is appropriate for children at particular developmental stages
- provide experiences that enhance all areas of the child's development
- respect and represent diversity in the selection of stories
- balance child/teacher-initiated learning
- value play as a critical aspect of development
- set up environments and materials to safely provide choices, involvement, and challenges for all children
- welcome partnerships with families in this process

and when the children

- experience a wealth of literacy opportunities
- feel comfortable and confident to explore their environment in novel ways
- have access to materials that speak to their needs
- can explore a story over time
- have a family member or friend who can share or extend the story experience at home
- are supported as they learn to interact and communicate with their peers in an inclusive setting

The journey starts with a story as the common experience and encourages all team members to read and know the story well. How it is played out in the course of its life in any setting depends on the players. The atmosphere that is established during the planning of a journey is one of learning, relating, and enjoying. The team involvement is a vital part of the journey process as children, parents, therapists, and educators can contribute their unique ideas and expertise to help bring the story to life. The emphasis is on the story and how we can introduce it into the children's play and world knowledge. Ties to curriculum areas are important, but they are not to take over and make "work" out of children's play. The suggested starting place is a discussion of the story (its main themes, special aspects, appeal) and a brainstorming of ideas that will link facets of the story to the lives of children and the classroom domains. The idea is to organize and plan the experiences in the setting around the story theme, to link the plan and the story in a way that will prime the developmental pump for the children, and to gather the necessary props and materials for the facilitation of ideas. The connections to home and community play an important role. When families are a part of the process, children experience the enriching and vital daily life extensions of the stories beyond the classroom. One family, for example, acted out the three bears as part of its nightly routine for weeks beyond the children's classroom journey with the story. The parents watched their two children blossom—taking on different roles, changing the endings, and relishing the shared play time with Mom and Dad (especially when Dad was Goldilocks).

The journey probes new routes through a story by developing environments, selecting and extending the use of materials, and exploring unique ways to link the story concepts to the various curriculum areas or relevant centers in a classroom. It is a rich mingling of dramatic play, sensory materials, blocks, art, science, manipulatives, books, and many other activities. The story props, project extensions, and reenactment setups are available throughout the environment as a resource or framework for story replay. They are usually novel arrangements of the available equipment and present invitations to play, explore, discover, and connect with others. The team partnerships between the teachers, support staff, families, and the child are a critical part of the total process. Stories are an excellent bridge linking the roads between classrooms and connecting home and school.

STORY SELECTION

The story to be explored can be a selection by the teacher or team, a parent's suggestion, or a child's request. It can also address a need that has surfaced either in the class, in the community, or at home. The selection process for stories varies according to how well we really know the particular group of children with whom we are working. The selection should be a balance of adult nudges and child choice. We do suggest beginning with simple themes before moving on to more complex ones. Nursery rhymes, for example, offer the ingredients young children so enjoy— the brevity, the nonsense, and the repetitive rhythm of the words. Beginning stories such as *Goodnight Moon*, *The Runaway Bunny*, *Oh Dear*, and *Caps for Sale* also have those vital characteristics, especially the repetition and the simple story line. This is particularly important in an inclusive setting where we want all children, especially those with disabilities, to gain the ability to reenact the less complicated rhymes or tales, giving all beginners a certain security in attempting the replay and a chance to practice with feelings of confidence. The children who grasp the meaning quickly will be given many opportunities to expand their own learning by choosing from an array of materials and environmental setups. It is not the story that "holds" children back, it is how that story is offered and what choices children feel free to make within their setting—either story-related or something they're engaged in that may have nothing to do with the story.

One teacher was particularly effective in using nursery rhymes in the fall with his first graders. The children felt like they were in familiar territory and could begin to "read" right away. They had so much fun acting out the rhymes that they decided to make costumes, then put on a show for the preschool in their building. The reception from the three- and four-year-olds was a real boost to their egos and encouraged them to read new stories to act out. Periodically they would take the stories they were working on and do "productions" for the preschool as an extension of the story. Another teacher effectively used *Alice in Wonderland* with her four- and five-year-olds. One of the children had brought the book to school one day and the teacher started reading it to a small group. The children in various parts of the room started to wander over until almost the whole class was listening. It eventually evolved into a journey of over a month. Some children were totally involved and stayed with "Alice" throughout, while a few of the children pursued other stories with a parent helper. The point is that the selection of stories for a journey must be based on your group, your spirit of adventure, your courage and commitment to take a risk, and your ability to balance deliberately the exposure to adults' knowledge with the interests and engagement of the children.

Sensitive Issues in the Selection Process

The bibliography in Chapter 10 contains stories we have categorized according to our experiences with them; these are merely suggestions of a simple-to-complex progression. As caregivers or teachers, we have the responsibility to select each book with much thought to its content and relevance to our particular children. We must be sensitive to how children might personalize a story we have selected. An awareness of the family situations, cultures, religions, and social biases of the "smaller community" in our classrooms must be developed with respect as we choose which stories to tell. From the standpoint of families alone, we are a different world than we used to be. The days of a mother, a father, a brother, a sister, two dogs, and a cat are rare: Single parents, stepfamilies, gay families, and racially and culturally mixed families are more likely to be a part of our settings. Being aware of and sensitive to who in the children's lives will support them beyond the classroom is important.

In one classroom a kindergarten teacher read a story about policemen to a small group. The other children gathered to hear it and wanted to have a policeman come to the room. The children dictated a letter requesting a visit. The teacher gave the officer some idea of the origin of the request and what she felt the children wanted to hear. When it came time for questions at the end of his visit, one child asked: "Do you put kids in jail?" The policeman's answer was: "Don't you worry, son, we only put *bad* people in jail!" (The father of the little boy who asked the question *was* serving time!) Sometimes no matter how well we select stories or plan the visits of special people to extend on a story, there will be these poignant reminders that as a society we still have much to learn about human relationships, and in particular our sensitivity to what children are *really* asking us through their story selections and in real life!

WHAT MAKES THE STORYBOOK JOURNEY UNIQUE

So what makes the storybook journey any different from anyone else's use of children's literature in the classroom or at home? Perhaps it is the amount of time we spend on each story, the emphasis on the variety of ways for all children to experience the story repeatedly, the value given to children's play, or its successful use as an intervention strategy for challenged children. One workshop participant wrote in her evaluation: "The journey gives children a scaffold for holding and building on their own ideas. It provides teachers and the classroom team with a framework for developing a meaningful curriculum and planning with a renewed understanding of child development at the core of the curriculum and their particular children at the core of their planning." Paying keen attention to setting up environments to enhance story-related play is very important in the storybook journey process. It provides the means for inviting children to become engaged over time in a very personal way with the story and internalizing its meaning at a pace and in a style that is uniquely their own. The efforts and joys are supported, respected, and extended by caring, involved, responsible adults.

Years ago, a student shared a definition from *Joy of Cooking* (1946) that seems like a unique analogy to what we are doing: "Never underestimate the power of a marinade . . . marinades are a means of spreading flavor by immersion . . . the soaking period may vary from only a few minutes to many hours." The stories are our marinade. We immerse the children in stories and related meaningful activities. Some soak up the meaning quickly, while others need to soak it up for weeks, repeating for mastery, for love, or for a deeper comprehension. Children, when given a choice, will opt for their own forms of immersion. It is our task to offer them a variety of experiences and materials so that they can self-select their form and timing of marination. If we trust them, they will produce the ingredients they need to do the task at hand.

One of our parents shared just such a connection that had occurred at home. Her determined daughter, who had a language disability, went into the cardboard box that was fashioned into a house with doors, windows, curtains, and various other homelike trappings. Usually this child would offer a physical gesture or

A young child finds a quiet place to become immersed in a storybook.

"come in" command to her mother, and mom would enter into her play. This day, however, the door was slammed shut and the words were "no come in!" Mother knew we had done "The Three Little Pigs" in school a number of weeks before this, so on a hunch, she thought, "I'll give the wolf's message: 'Little pig, little pig, let me come in!'" The joyful giggly answer from the three-year-old piglet inside was: "No chin chin chin." Janie had been marinading in this story and now she could confidently and independently take control. The familiarity with the story for both mom and Janie helped Janie feel connected to her little social world at home. It was a secure world that accepted and supported her struggle and efforts to interact competently and with a real purpose.

One distinct difference may be the use of stories as a "social interaction" bridge linking children with disabilities and children who are typically developing. Sometimes children do not develop as nature had intended and their pursuit of the story is hampered by the challenges and frustrations of a body whose movements they cannot control or a voice that cannot let the world know in words what they are thinking, feeling, or imagining. Challenged children must wait to have the world brought to them; playing in the mud while pretending to make the three pigs' brick house, walking on sand, or splashing in a puddle require help from an adult who not only values these experiences, but also has the physical strength to bring the child to that experience.

One teacher shared his concern about how to meaningfully include a little boy with disabilities in the group storytelling. Bret was unable to sit up unassisted and was confined to a special wheelchair. Unless lifted out, he was "trapped" in that environment and physically distanced from his peers. The teacher explained to the children what he was doing as he gently removed Bret from his chair and placed him on his lap. As they sat on the floor beside the other children, Bret slid out flat and seemed to be indicating he wanted to lie down on his back. The teacher respected this request, made him as comfortable as possible, and went on telling about the three pigs. He kept an eye on Bret and moved the book around so that he could see the story. The teacher could not tell from Bret's expression or body posture whether Bret was really involved with the story at any level. When the wolf and the group huffed and puffed to blow the house down, Bret used every bit of strength in the muscles of his tiny mouth to pucker up and blow that house down, too. The teacher was amazed and touched to see that he really had followed along, knew when to huff and puff, and used all that stamina to join in the group telling. The accomplishment was celebrated and Bret sensed he was part of the action. He was able to show us his inner involvement through this very vivid outward gesture. He was so much more motivated to participate when he was out of his wheelchair and close enough to his peers to feel a part of the action.

In an inclusive setting, the adults also need to provide interactional invitations to the children whose emotional stability has been invaded by stress or genetics and to those who struggle with mental difficulties limiting their degree of comprehension. Many children have trouble staying focused and engaged or finding the stamina to pursue learning on their own. The journey provides pitons for many of these children to hang onto as they learn to communicate and interact around a shared experience. The story encourages dialogue and turn taking in various forms because the subject is held in common and the communication in context. For example, the story of "The Three Bears" contains a progression of meaningful activities: The bears go out into the woods, allowing their porridge to cool; while they're gone, a certain blond visitor goes into their house as an uninvited guest, and so on. For children with limited comprehension, speech/language, hearing or articulation difficulties, the repeated and varied experiences with the story and the reenactment with their peer models give them a common ground. They all know what comes next and by choice can be part of the action in a social context. Even if it is only by wearing furry ears, stomping through the pretend woods, and testing the homemade porridge with the other bears, the story has meaning for all at various levels.

 For young Zach it provided an entry into a small group. He had decided to be Goldilocks and speedily went through the motions of getting into the bears' house, eating, sitting in chairs, and going up to bed—all without words. The teacher assisted by narrating off to one side. When the bears returned and eventually got to the bedroom, they all stopped by baby bear's bed where "Goldilocks" lay sleeping. There was absolute silence! The teacher suggested that maybe the bears could growl. Growl they did and "Goldilocks-Zach" sat straight up in bed with a scrunched-up face, his hands out like claws. To our surprise, he growled back! The bears went running off and Zach paraded around as if he were the proud new owner of a bear's house. For this child who normally did not play effectively with others, and who struggled to process information, it was a powerful moment of communication through playing out a well-loved story with a very novel twist at the end!

For children to act out a part, they need other people. Role taking in a commonly known story becomes an effective nudge toward communicating and cooperating with another person. Interactions and role taking encourage children to "try on" the perspective of others. The practice of taking parts also helps the child to expand beyond the self to others in the safety of a role.

The stories told in this chapter were taken from inclusive/integrated settings in which the children were at the very basic level of learning to be human to each other. They were just beginning to notice and care about differences among people, and, more importantly, they were starting to accept and try new ways of interacting and connecting with each other. Those of us who have been using the journey for a number of years believe that the human-to-human interactions fostered through our enjoyment, common knowledge, and exploration over time of a known story are perhaps its most rewarding aspect.

Meaningful inclusion is a process for all of us—children, educators, and families. The adults in each setting are challenged to make the philosophy a reality by sincerely valuing and modeling what they believe. We, as educators, need to start very early in a child's life to include *all* children and their families into our settings regardless of race, abilities, cultural heritage, or other qualities that might have segregated us in the past. Beyond just including people, we want to support and nurture each others' attempts to interact sensitively and meaningfully. Young children can teach us so much about how to do this! We watched a child spontaneously reach out and put Red Riding Hood's cape on a peer who was confined to a rolling bed so she could go along with the group to "grandma's" house. We sat among a group of children who were genuinely thrilled when their three-year-old classmate (who had never spoken to them before) said "fish" while they were looking at the book, *Swimmy*, together. We observed the child who invented her own sign language with a hearing impaired child so she could communicate with him at the

Beyond just including children, we want to support and nurture their attempts to interact and communicate.

easel they were sharing. We saw a little girl hold her hands out in a protective gesture behind an unsteady classmate who was trying to walk through "the forest" with the rest of the class. That's what the human-to-human process is all about! When sincere compassion and caring are modeled at home and in school, children are very capable of reaching beyond self. By sharing their commitment and deep caring for children, adults free children to care for each other. The story provides a way to act upon their feelings and to practice in small, but vitally important ways, the essence of being human.

In summary, the storybook journey process is unique in each setting. At its core are human relationships, an emphasis on the value of play, the creation of both the physical and psychological environment, and the development and use of materials. The journey develops these four aspects as the foundation, children as the most valuable resource, and storybooks as a vehicle to help integrate their learning. These are the central ripples in the journey "pool," and jumping in takes a very real commitment to children and their families. When mastered with a keen knowledge of how children develop and learn, the storybook journey provides pathways to literacy through life and play experiences.

*P*lay as a process lies at the very core of human behavior and development.

~Urie Bronfenbrenner

The Human Expedition

The Effect of Children's Play on Development

This chapter will

- *Link the following core areas of development to play:*

P = Physical development

L = Language and learning (cognitive development)

A = Affective (emotional development) and

Y = Yourself in relation to others (social development)

PLAY AND THE CHILD

Being passionate about something unleashes the energy to persist and the necessary creativity to attempt to master and accomplish what is important to us. Play for the child is passion, intensity, and the wholehearted experience of living. It is an energizer and organizer to the young child's feelings and way of thinking. Just watch the child who runs from the water spigot to the end of the hose he has just buried in his experimental sand volcano. There is wonder, anticipation, and excitement in every part of his body. For those who have helped him heap the sand over the end of the hose, that pervasive spirit becomes contagious. The collaborative problem solving is a dynamic part of the play and a social function of learning.

Play is what young children want to do! Seldom, if ever, do we need to show children how to play with a toy or a cardboard box. If we've endowed them with the courage to risk and have not squelched their sense of wonder, they'll find a way because they want to, they're curious, their pursuit is self-initiated, and because it is an enjoyable thing to do. Adults, often with the best of intentions and sometimes because they can't resist "playing" themselves, feel a need to demonstrate how to use a toy before a child has the chance to explore alone. This interaction often becomes an interference with the child's chosen style of exploring and learning. If we are to gain a real understanding of the child through play, it would be wise for us to observe the child's initial pursuit of the materials and human interactions before we interrupt with our own agenda. Easier said than done, but critical to our gaining a comprehensive look at the child, is our ability to observe quietly and to facilitate interaction when appropriate. To "teach" play is to negate the very essence of its spontaneity and self-driven origin. Thank goodness most young children will make it dramatically obvious to us if we are interfering in their play: They either protest with noise or they get up and leave. A child's mode of communication is more physical, as words are not yet the most comfortable means of expression. This demands that we tune in to nonverbal body language to help us interpret what that body might be saying as the child engages in play. All of us have seen the child who smiles at us with his lips, but his eyes and awkward body poses tell us something quite different.

LINKING THE CORE AREAS OF DEVELOPMENT TO PLAY

Physical Play and Sensory Integration with Stories

Children in the early years are active agents and participants in life. Their play is a continuous exploration using their bodies and senses: hearing, seeing, touching, feeling, tasting, smelling. Play becomes the vehicle to integrate all the senses and provides an opportunity to begin organizing that sensory input for later use. A. Jean Ayres (1979) developed the theory of sensory integration while doing her postdoctoral work at the Brain Research Institute at the University of California–Los Angeles. Dr. Ayres theorized that our basic senses are closely allied and form interconnections with other systems of the brain as development proceeds. The interplay among the various senses is complex and is necessary for a person to interpret a situation accurately and respond appropriately. *Sensory integration* is the term used to refer to this organization of the senses. Ayres (1972) wrote that the ability to communicate is an end-product of the sensory integration process. This has had a profound effect on the training of both the occupational therapist and the speech pathologist as they study the interrelationship of sensory integration processing and speech-language development. As teachers, caregivers, and parents, a knowledge of this theory and its implications will help guide our work with children and the environmental considerations in their play. Providing children a rich selection of raw materials and physical pursuits to explore helps them begin to see beyond their eyes and feel with more than their hands. A child moving through space and planning how to get off, on, around, and through various pieces of equipment, maintaining balance, and feeling safe reveals the complexity and interrelated aspects of the senses. Play and story reenactments provide excellent trappings for physical and sensory activities and a means for the observant adult to heed the warning signs of a child having trouble in this critical aspect of development.

The occupational therapist on our team has really caught the spirit of the Storybook Journey and brought so much more depth to our understanding of physical development. She has transformed ropes into bean stalks and regular climbers into triple decker bunk beds for the three bears. Introducing the three layers of beds not only reignited and inspired delightful reenactments of the story, but it also gave us a grand opportunity to watch the various children go about climbing, motor planning, and coping with the world from new perspectives. One little girl got under the lower bunk just fine, but when it came time to get out she was totally disoriented and seemed to freeze. One never knows in such a case if the emotional gate is closing off any problem-solving skills at a time like this or if she perhaps just didn't have the repertoire of movement to experiment with getting herself out of this space. It wasn't until she started to cry that we realized she really saw herself as permanently lodged in that position. We talked her through moving her body in different positions, head down, crunching, and so forth, and she was finally free. When we shared this vignette with her mother at the end of the day, she said that was a frequent occurrence at home. Lori would crawl under the coffee table in their living room, turn around, sit on her bottom, peer out at the world, and then would panic, having no idea how to get out. This shared information was extremely valuable in our pursuit of ways to provide experiences for Lori both at school and at home.

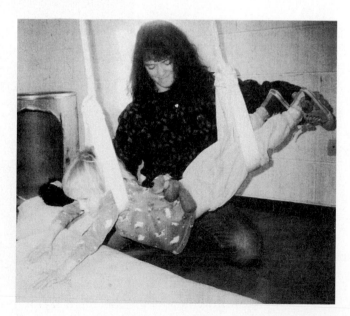

Play and story reenactments provide excellent opportunities for physical and sensory activities and/or therapy in the classroom. Here, a child is "flying" like Wendy in Peter Pan.

Language and Learning Through Play with Stories

Play allows children to combine their fragmented information gathering by seeking connections and relationships through direct contact with their world. Children are searching for clarification and personal meaning, and they will develop best if they are given the time to learn through their own interests, the choice of a wide variety of experiences, and the right to pursue this learning in a style and at a pace that will serve them best. According to Zeity (1974),

> Play is central to learning for young children. It reflects the individual child's perception of the relationships in his world. In play children integrate knowledge, skills, and feelings. The teachers respect and support play by building it into their curriculum. They listen to the language of play, and then provide new opportunities and accessory materials which help children elaborate their ideas. Increasingly, the work of individuals becomes related to the work of others and cooperative projects are undertaken. The group process in turn serves to stimulate and generate individual thought and development. Within this classroom the teachers help each child use language to express and fulfill his desires, to formulate questions and ideas, to exchange meaning with others. Words are presented as useful and fun. Children are encouraged to experiment with them as a natural process of communication. Thus the children are enabled to integrate their thinking, their language use, and the mastery of symbolic skills in a situation which is known and guided by supportive adults. (p. 2)

 Play is the having and sharing of wonderful ideas. It is the practice grounds for communication. While observing in a child care center one day, my attention was drawn to the dramatic play corner, where a group of about four children were busily involved in a domestic scene:

The teacher listens intently as this child shares the meaning of what he has drawn in his journal.

Laticha:	"Can I play in your house with you?"
The Group:	"No!"
Laticha:	"I could be the sister."
Javad:	"No, we gotta sister."
Laticha:	"I could be the dog."
The Group:	"We gotta dog."

Laticha wandered away and slumped in a chair a few feet away. "The group" watched and then went on playing. Javad kept looking over at Laticha—he appeared to be struggling with group dynamics and compassion for his friend, Laticha. Finally, Javad yelled out: "You could be the next door neighbor." Laticha leaped out of her chair, yelled back "okay," and immediately started to build an extension to the structure the group had built. The first thing she moved into her house was a phone.

Communication occurs to the extent that one's thoughts and feelings are understood by another. This brief vignette, encompassing so much, revealed the inclusive and integrative value of play. There was compassion, having and exchanging ideas, problem solving, risk taking, rejection, verbal communication, body language, and a resolution that satisfied everyone's needs for the moment. Playing out the various themes in the course of the journey process also provides a unique practice ground for the children to develop not only a better understanding of each other, but also an understanding of the world around them. "The greater the child's repertoire of action and thoughts, the more materials he has for trying to put things together in his head" (Elkind, 1987).

 In our center, *The Very Hungry Caterpillar* provided just the means to move our thinking and world knowledge along in complexity from the concrete to the abstract. The story idea of the caterpillar eating a variety of things in abundance, then spinning his cocoon, became a reality as the children observed our collection of live caterpillars eating the dill leaves and spinning their special places for transformation. The children were nudged into extending their concepts and fitting new information into their original schema, by inching along like a caterpillar and using colorful scarves to envelop their bodies as they spun into "cocoons." They further internalized the experience by opening up the scarves and flapping them as wings as the caterpillar had metamorphosed into a butterfly. Sensing the freedom and movement of themselves as newly launched butterflies, they could more concretely experience the process of change.

Emotional Growth Through Play with Stories

"In his everyday life play is the child's natural form of expression, a language that brings him into a communicating relationship with others and with the world in which he lives. Through play he learns the meaning of things and the relation between objects—and himself; and in play he provides himself with a medium of motor activity and emotional expression" (Allen, 1942). Frederick Allen, through his close work with the wounded child, knew the value of play as a vehicle for children to express their thoughts and feelings; play is a way to test reality that is safely masked in fantasy.

This very hungry caterpillar has just emerged from the cocoon and is fluttering around to dry her wings.

 It is just such fantasy that allowed Betsy to yell: "I can too scream because I am the mother screaming for you to stop screaming!" How wonderful for this four-year-old to explain to "her child" (and vicariously to the teacher) that she was "safely" screaming at her child in play to try on that role of control, power, and mother figure in her sociodramatic enactment of something she has either lived with or observed elsewhere. Play is powerful. Becoming the "Bad Guy"—the wolf, troll, doctor, or in this case, the yelling mother—is vital to emotional development. Through the magic and escape of replay, young children begin to learn to manage their feelings and affective responses. To feel in control in a rather scary world—even if only momentarily—is a catharsis. The child's role playing can provide us with a small window into his perception of the world; however, we do not always readily understand what we see and hear in play.

The story can play such a valuable role in this emotional catharsis. It can often provide the structure or safe framework within which the child can gain an awareness of or perhaps even begin to work through some unsettling feelings.

 Jessie's reaction to the reading and acting out of *Little Red Riding Hood* is equally powerful. Jessie's mother died during Jessie's infancy and she had always called the grandmother who raised her "Mommy." In our reenactment of the story, every time Little Red Riding Hood took the basket of goodies from "Mommy" to give to "Grandma," Jessie left the group and paced anxiously in another section of the room or looked outside through the glass door with her back to the group. Perhaps the awareness on Jessie's part that Mommy was separate from

Grandma in this story was very unsettling and her withdrawal from the flurry of activity a significant step in her attempt to assimilate this information on a very personal level. Our observations also gave us a tangible example that we could share with Jessie's grandparents and father of the struggle this little girl was experiencing. To help Jessie work through the process of understanding what had really happened in her young life, it was critical for the family and the staff to find a way to bridge the gap with her. In this case, something very special happened! Both Jessie's maternal and paternal grandparents brought out pictures of Jessie's mother (even one treasured picture of Jessie being held by her mother). Together we made a book about Jessie's entrance into life, the death of her mother, her family now, and her days at school. This homemade book was a real catharsis for all of us, but it appeared most effective in helping the grandparents realize that Jessie needed this information to begin to work through some of her deepest feelings. Like so many of us, they were trying to protect Jessie from the very thing she needed to know most: the truth. Little Red Riding Hood played a significant role for all of us!

Social Relationships Through Play with Stories

Emotional and social development are often discussed together because they are uniquely tied. In this chapter, we're looking at the areas separately, but the core areas for all development are deeply interwoven. Play provides unequaled opportunities as it is the fertile soil in which the social aspects of development can grow. I like to call the child's very early attempts at this process *social bumping*. Take, for example, the children who topple off their cardboard block wall, pretending to be Humpty Dumpty. They are naturally landing in close proximity of each other and are thus in playful physical contact. For very young, developmentally challenged, or shy children, this may spark one of their first social interactions away from home at a very primitive level. It reminds one of puppies wagging their tails and circling each other. Igor Gamow (1987) shares another example:

> One characteristic of penguins is that large groups of them mill around the edge of the water off some very icy platform and while they are milling they are also actively bumping into one another until finally one gets bumped into the water. The moment one of the penguins gets bumped in, all the rest stop milling and bumping and observe the penguin which is now "in the drink," and if that penguin is not eaten by a leopard seal they all jump in. (p. 25)

Although Igor makes quite a different point in his article, I'd like to use his penguin pushing and the tail wagging as examples that can likewise relate to children's social probing. Children use this shared bumping and circling behavior as a way to check out a possible friendly encounter. Depending on whether the encounter was enjoyable and accepted, they will either repeat the activity or move on and watch. This preverbal social bumping is a beginning point of social interaction and communication and progresses into the very complex process of human relations. Katz (1987) notes:

> Although definitions of social competence vary on some of the details, they generally include the capacity to initiate, develop, and maintain satisfying relationships with others, especially peers. Social competence does not require a child to be a social butterfly. It is not a source of concern if a child chooses to work or play alone, as long as he or she is capable of interacting productively and successfully with another when desired or when appropriate.

Children can use the props of a story to make social connections. Sharing hats while acting out Caps for Sale *really became more important than the story itself.*

 Dylan was a young boy who, for the first three months of school, was unable to become involved with others beyond fleeting eye contact. For weeks he physically and emotionally isolated himself from his peers and the adults in his center. His behavior was a red flag, as he not only was unable to initiate interactions, but on a far deeper level, he also showed no desire to be a part of anything taking place around him. He was a social isolate in every sense of the word. It was only through the talented support of the patient, watchful, understanding staff in combination with Dylan's growing trust in his world and self that he was able to reach out, first to the consistent adults in his life and finally to the children. Peter Pan became the intermediator, providing Dylan with the means to experience the world through the safety of walking in someone else's shoes. The story of *Peter Pan* became the vicarious tester of the social process . . . the substance for acting out feelings through a storybook character . . . the vehicle for moving toward others. As Dylan began to gain a sense of himself and an awareness of and interest in his peers, he slowly accepted them into his story-related play. Though they "flew" with him as Peter Pan in a very associative stage of socialization in the beginning, they later invited him into their play as a cooperative member of other story reenactments. He grew into a child who could comfortably balance his quiet times alone with his newly developed social competence in maintaining satisfying reciprocal relationships in play.

The use of stories as the core of our program plays a very significant role in the social development and communicative competence of young children. Socially, the story provides children with a central focus and common knowledge of a scenario to play out with predictable characters and sequenced situations. The story line is a scaffold providing each child with a vehicle for becoming an active, playful participant at a variety of cognitive, linguistic, social, and emotional levels with feedback from peers serving as a social reinforcement. In the context of the story, children can be encouraged to communicate. Since everyone in the group is familiar with the story, the more verbal children can carry the essence of the plot. The less verbal children can fill in or chant "trip trap, trip trap" as they master the words through joyful repetition, practice, and peer acceptance. The children's sense of being a part of the interaction enhances their learning and helps them to identify more closely with their peers. When Papa Bear is one of the less verbal children, he can go through the motions while being encouraged by a more verbal Mama: "Come on Papa, we're going upstairs." Papa hears the language, follows the other bears and becomes part of the social context.

Through our keen observations of children's play and our meaningful partnerships with parents, we will begin to see how each child is progressing from egocentrism to a sense of self in relation to others. Children's uniqueness and individuality will begin to take form as they construct their own styles of relating. Their techniques for approaching one another successfully are important as are the feelings involved in the approach of others. Cooperation, collaboration, negotiation, and the intense and passionate pursuit of friendships will be an ongoing process.

Play is children's most useful tool for preparing themselves for the future and its tasks. Flexible thinking, communication, transformations, combinations, fantasies, emotional stresses and delights, human relationships, compassion, movement, and creative pursuits all occur in play. Children advance into new stages of mastery through play, practice, and the pursuit of their own interests. Spontaneous play is development, and development for the young child *is* play.

VISUALIZING PLAY AND DEVELOPMENTAL LINKS

For those of us who are more visual, it might help to think about the links between development and play if we see them in a graphic form (see Figures 2–1 and 2–2). Each letter of play will be assigned a corresponding core area of development. A concise review will then emerge of what children tell us about their individuality through play.

P will stand for physical development and the child's desire to be an active agent and participant in life. Young children are integrated, moving beings who want to see, smell, hear, and touch all parts of their expanding world to internalize all of its dimensions. Their bodies carry emotional messages and communicate their feelings in an unspoken language. They want to master challenges and control their developing muscles through repetitive, intense physical play.

L will stand for learning and language to signify cognition. The L pertains to children's innate and unquenchable drive to understand the world and to gain freedom and competence in it. Children want to be engaged participants in their own learning. The span of time we are touching on is Piaget's preoperational period of approximately two to seven years of age. This is a prelogical stage of thinking at which children are egocentric, perception-bound, and intuitive. Their learning is a random doing, undoing, and redoing of their world through play. The power of language is intense and the desire to communicate, vital.

A is to represent affective or emotional development and the critical role of self-esteem in children's struggles to grow as whole persons. Young children are moving through the first three stages (trust, autonomy, and initiation) of Erikson's eight stages of human growth. They are gaining a sense of self and discovering whether their worth is confirmed or denied through human relationships and their surrounding environment.

There has been a surge of developmental research on the emotional life of children that reveals the intimate interplay between the affective and cognitive aspects of a child's life. Dr. T. Barry Brazelton (1984), a Harvard University researcher and

Figure 2–1
Selected ingredients of development

	Selected Ingredients of Development
P = Physical Development	Coordination of sensory and motor activity Maturation/experience Sensory input/sensory integration Refining skills Body control/movement Activity level Developmental patterns Special influences (e.g., race, ethnic backgrounds, environment, deprivation) Body language
L = Language and Learning (Cognitive Development)	Sensorimotor—preoperational period Individual pace/style Concept formation Random learning/intuitive leaps/risk taking Disruption-reorganization-integration Schema development (way of organizing thought/mental sketch of how the world works) Communication Language acquisition Verbal play/rhymes/rhythms Investigating word combinations/power of words Egocentric/perspective bound/perception bound
A = Affective (Emotional Development)	Trust/autonomy/initiative Hope/will/purpose Sense of self Relationships/genuine human contact Role of personal experience Value (confirm/deny) Creating emotional ideas/thinking Engagement/frustration level/attention Behavior toward self/others
Y = Yourself in Relation to Others (Social Development)	Eye contact (aware of cultural differences) Meaningful interactions Role of temperament (adult and child) Significant early relationships Continuing significance of relationships Egocentrism/altruism Constructing a style of relating Emotional links—attachment Cognitive links—understanding/grasp of certain concepts Social milieu of family, peers Uniqueness/individuality

Figure 2–1 *(continued)*

Play	Enhancement of Development Through Story
P = Physical Development	Inclusion of all senses Active participation/hands-on Movement as a primary inroad to all learning/integration Physical nudges through role playing Physical nudges through environmental set ups Encourages perceptual—motor skills Testing limits Risk taking Relaxation through stories
L = Language and Learning (Cognitive Development)	Repetition for mastery over time Energizer/organizer of learning Planning—problem solving—decisions Memory—sequence—invention—imagination Concentration/focused attention/engagement Construct—deconstruct—reconstruct Power of language/encourages dialogues A framework for communication Movement combined with speech Transformations Experientially based pursuit Creative/unique approach Language taught in a meaningful context/shared information Novel in context of familiar
A = Affective (Emotional Development)	Emotional release/growth/catharsis Fantasy/reality bridge Relive experiences/explore feelings Test limits Wish fulfillment Mastery/gain control/power Freedom to make mistakes/rules are suspended in play Verify self-worth
Y = Yourself in Relation to Others (Social Development)	Practice field for social learning/perspective taking Concept of the world—morals, manners, gender roles, etc. Bilingual sharing Empathy through different roles Test ideas and behavior Stimulates stages from observer to cooperative play Communication in a social context Reality testing Contagious quality Language as social power Practice—modify—compromise Turn taking Group time Role taking

Figure 2–2
Play and its link to development

P =
Physical Development

_____

L =
Language and Learning
(Cognitive
Development)

_____

A =
Affective (Emotional
Development)

_____

Y =
Yourself in Relation to
Others (Social
Development)

popular author on child development, expressed: "It's about time we started looking at emotions more carefully. Everything we know about a child shows that healthy emotional development is the key to other kinds of growth."

Stanley Greenspan and his wife, Nancy Thorndike Greenspan, have written an excellent book, *First Feelings*. One of the great contributions of this book is their clear development of the theory that intellectual and emotional development cannot be separated. Many examples of this theory will be woven into this journey.

Y, with its "arms" outstretched, will stand for yourself in relation to others or social development. How one constructs a style of relating to others will have implications for life. It has much to do with the role of temperament, the impact of those critical early relationships, and the child's health. The uniqueness and individuality of each child will be revealed in how they negotiate relationships as a leader, follower, team player, collaborator, and the like.

Figure 2–1 outlines a unique framework for the important play/development connection and the incorporation and enhancement of both play and development through the storybook journey. Pulling play apart in such a fashion may give you the false illusion that children's play falls neatly into little categories for easy observational assessment. Not true! Children's novel approach to life makes us realize that we can't put anything about their development in such a neat categorical box. Experienced observation of children at play only makes us realize how inseparable and intertwined play really is with all aspects of development. It would make as much sense to look at cognitive aspects of play detached from all the other core areas of development as it would to spell the word play with only two of its four letters. The P-L-A-Y chart (Figure 2–1) is merely an abbreviated short course to quickly impart the idea of connectedness and the visual link for the philosophical foundation for the storybook journey.

If space allowed, the chart would have larger sections so you could continuously add your own thoughts, references, and observations. The blank P-L-A-Y chart (Figure 2–2) is one way you can record your own play/development links as an extension to what has already been provided. It has also been used at parent conference time with both the teacher and the parents filling out each area for a child and then comparing notes at conference time. It is particularly helpful if parents are questioning the value of play.

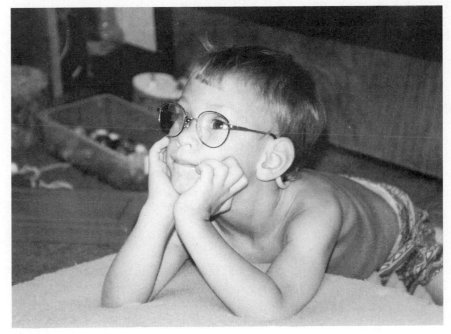

E ngagement with a task in hand will lead to self-motivation and results from a conviction that the task is worth doing, is possible to achieve, and will not have unpleasant consequences.

~Brian Cambourne

A Philosophical Guide

Brian Cambourne's Condition of Learning Applied to the Storybook Journey

This chapter will

provide the philosophical underpinnings of the storybook journey using the conditions of Brian Cambourne's model of literacy learning as a framework. The seven conditions are immersion, demonstration, expectation, responsibility, use, approximation, and response. Figure 3–1 represents this model within the context of literacy learning.

*I*n Andrea Butler's and Jan Turnbill's *Towards a Reading-Writing Classroom* (1987), a chapter by Brian Cambourne ("Language, Learning, and Literacy") identifies seven primary conditions that are relevant to all kinds of learning. These conditions provide the unique hitching post on which to tie the philosophical underpinnings of the storybook journey process. I will redefine each condition to illustrate how the storybook journey supports building foundations for literacy development in young children. Suggestions for implementation are listed under each condition.

Immersion

- Slides from a book
- Character dress-up
- Draw, paint, or cutout a story
- Overhead projector story
- Clay characters
- Adult/child reenactments
- Word play
- Use of nature

Demonstration

- Recipe reading
- Imitation
- Real connections
- Model reading

Expectations

- Peer significance
- Finding a way to participate
- Deeper understanding
- What do adults expect

Responsibility

- Teacher's role
- The parent's role
- Ideas to support parent efforts
- The child's role

Use

- Exposure to story language
- Real-life experiences
- Individual comfort levels in the use of stories

Approximation

- Meaningful beginnings
- Special events
- A child's approximation and the teacher's extension

Response/Feedback

- Adult-to-child response
- Child-to-child response

Figure 3–1
A schematic representation of Brian Cambourne's model of learning as it applies to literacy learning

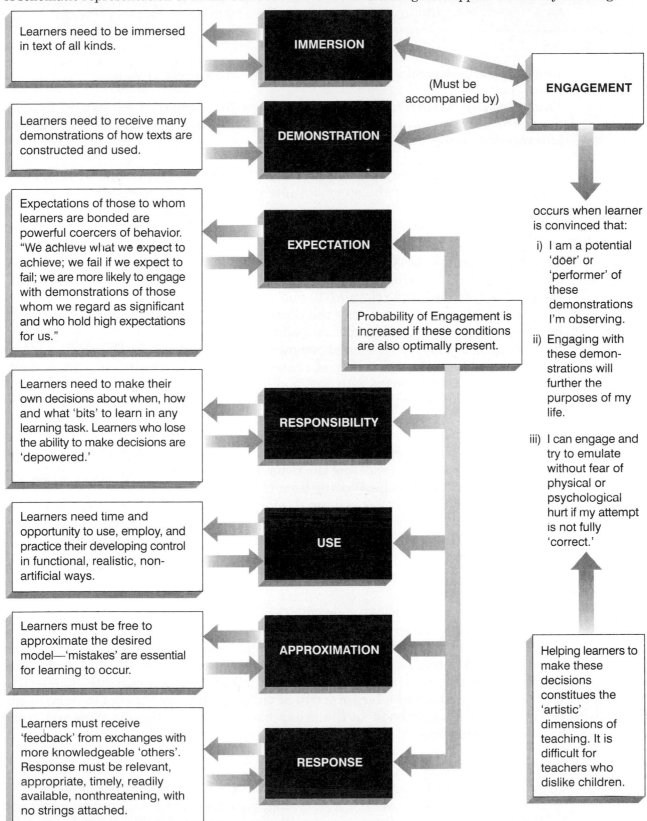

Learners need to be immersed in text of all kinds.

Learners need to receive many demonstrations of how texts are constructed and used.

Expectations of those to whom learners are bonded are powerful coercers of behavior. "We achieve what we expect to achieve; we fail if we expect to fail; we are more likely to engage with demonstrations of those whom we regard as significant and who hold high expectations for us."

Learners need to make their own decisions about when, how and what 'bits' to learn in any learning task. Learners who lose the ability to make decisions are 'depowered.'

Learners need time and opportunity to use, employ, and practice their developing control in functional, realistic, non-artificial ways.

Learners must be free to approximate the desired model—'mistakes' are essential for learning to occur.

Learners must receive 'feedback' from exchanges with more knowledgeable 'others'. Response must be relevant, appropriate, timely, readily available, nonthreatening, with no strings attached.

IMMERSION

DEMONSTRATION

EXPECTATION

RESPONSIBILITY

USE

APPROXIMATION

RESPONSE

ENGAGEMENT

(Must be accompanied by)

Probability of Engagement is increased if these conditions are also optimally present.

occurs when learner is convinced that:

i) I am a potential 'doer' or 'performer' of these demonstrations I'm observing.

ii) Engaging with these demonstrations will further the purposes of my life.

iii) I can engage and try to emulate without fear of physical or psychological hurt if my attempt is not fully 'correct.'

Helping learners to make these decisions constitues the 'artistic' dimensions of teaching. It is difficult for teachers who dislike children.

Source: From *The Whole Story* by B. Cambourne, 1988, Auckland, New Zealand: Ashton Scholastic.

- Meaningful involvement to feedback
- Home-school feedback loop

IMMERSION

Immersion allows children to experience a story in a variety of ways.

Surrounding children with many choices for repeated exposure, experience, and immersion with all aspects of a story is really at the heart of the storybook journey.

Immersion in one story over a period of time builds a certain comfort level and a deeper understanding of the story. Its intent is to encourage children's desire to revisit the story on their own using many different modalities for retelling, repeating, and reliving its magic. Hearing the story told and having it read while looking at the pictures are still perhaps the two most powerful ways to experience the essence of a story. In an address to the American Library Association in 1987, Geree H. Pawl said: " . . . when books come into one's life in the context of human warmth, nurturance, and relevance to one's own interests and needs, they maintain this quality forever. It is not only the characters in a book that engage our shared humanness—the book itself somehow becomes a companion. . . . "

In today's world, television and commercial videos often take the place of storytelling or reading. Though many of these videos are delightful and indeed have their place, we need to share with our families the value of daily time spent reading together. Research says that 15 minutes a day spent quietly reading with our children has powerful ramifications for a literate future. One teacher shared that when she reads *Goodnight Moon* to her young class she can still vividly remember how she snuggled up to her mother to hear this story read over and over again. All the images of her own room, repeating the ritual of saying goodnight to everything, and the feel of her soft quilt come floating back to memory.

We can provide many extensions to storytelling to help children master and enjoy stories on their own, with peers, or to be exposed to through the adults in their lives. The following are ideas adults can bring to the story time to add some unique variations and approaches to immersion in the storytelling experience.

Slides from a Book

Using one of the classic books your children enjoy, take a slide of every page. (This can also be done commercially, but it is very costly!) A darkened part of the room can become your "theater" with children bringing their chairs, rugs, pillows, and so on to watch the book flash up on the screen. As you show the slides of each page, the group can tell, read, or share the story together. This is a particularly effective way to "read" a story to a larger group of children. It is also a way to enlarge the pictures from a small book so the group can experience the pictures and story together without frustration.

Character Dress-up

Dress up as one of the characters from the book you are doing for the week. You might, for example, don overalls, a straw hat, big boots, and a neckerchief when you do *Old McDonald Had a Farm*; or wear all green and big swim flippers when you do

Frog and Toad Are Friends. Greet the children at the door and enjoy the diversity of reactions that you'll elicit from the children, their families, and even the bus driver! It's a fun way to weave the story into your day, right from the first "good mornings."

Draw, Paint, or Cut Out a Story

The adult can either draw, paint, or cut out a story alone or make it a joint venture with the children. In one center, the children painted a large mural in tones of green, blues, and yellow. The teacher stretched this across a wall and used it as the backdrop for telling the story of *Swimmy*. On separate pieces of tagboard, the teacher drew pictures of the lobster, eel, and other characters. As Swimmy swam along and met each character, they were placed on the backdrop with a small piece of tic tac (the sticky stuff—easily removed—used to adhere pictures to the wall). Each child had made red fish to stick up at random. When it was time to form the big fish with Swimmy as the eye, the teacher created the image with the children's red fish. If the props are left out, children can use them at their leisure to lay out *Swimmy* on their own or with a group. Children can also do all the drawings and place them up on the mural when their character is named.

Overhead Projector Story

Place a blank overhead plastic sheet on the glass of the projector. Use a pool of cooking oil on the sheet as the substance to hold the food coloring drops. This works particularly well for the story of *Little Blue and Little Yellow* by Leo Lionni. Drop the food coloring from an eye dropper onto the oil as you introduce yellow, blue, and their friends, red, purple, and the rest of the gang. Of course, when yellow and blue "hug" each other little green emerges. It is really quite magical and makes the "blob characters" seem real.

Playdoh Characters

Using the story of *Little Blue and Little Yellow* again, the teacher can make up Playdoh balls in both yellow and blue. A bit of each color Playdoh should be reserved to use later in the story. As she tells the story, the teacher would combine the blue and yellow balls, kneading them until they turn green (as they do in the story when they hug). The reserved yellow and blue balls are then used to form the part of the story where "the blobs" cry because their families don't understand who these "green" children could be. When they cry, yellow cries yellow Playdoh tears and blue cries blue Playdoh tears. They each pull themselves back together (the teacher collects the yellow tears she's made into a yellow blob, likewise the blue) and run home to their respective families.

Adult/Child Reenactments

Acting out a story with adults is a delightful first step to acting out a story with peers. For many children with varying abilities, the support of an adult is comforting as they take on a character role for the first time. Offering an invitation to join in by extending a hand, wheeling a child into the pretend forest, or supporting a child's attempts to participate is important. When we acted out *Where the Wild Things Are* with our painted faces and/or masks it was hard to tell the children from the adults during the wild rumpus (other than by our size). Even the most reluctant became caught up in the fun of it!

For many children, it is comforting and fun to have the support of an adult as they take on a character role for the first time. This reenactment involves placing wet vinyl bears on plexiglass.

Word Play

Some stories lend themselves to dramatizing some of the words, concepts, or feelings. It's a very simple form of immersion. An example might be some of the following from *Corduroy*. Take the word *escalator*. Say it with your pitch going up on esca- then down with -lator. Try saying *sad* as if you were sad like Lisa was when she couldn't take Corduroy home on the day she found him. Say *mommy* in two ways: as if you were very angry or mad at her for not letting you buy Corduroy or as happy when mommy let you take him home. Saying the title of some stories with feeling is an interesting experience: *Alexander and the Terrible, Horrible, No Good, Very Bad Day*; or saying *Swimmy* in a short, clipped way like darting fish ("swimmy", "swimmy," "swimmy"); or *King Bidgood's in the Bathtub* (say it like bubbles with loose, puffed cheeks).

Use of Nature

In the story *Mousekin and the Golden House*, a discarded Halloween pumpkin becomes a mouse's wonderful winter home. Since we had pet mice in our classroom one year, we took our used jack-o'-lantern and put it in our mouse's cage. It made the story come alive when our mouse did exactly what Mousekin did: She ran inside, ate the seeds, and pulled in everything she could to make her winter nest.

We also brought in a big spider to see if he'd spin a web as the spider had done in one of our favorite stories, *The Busy Spider*. For two days we watched in our aquarium, but no web. On the third day, the spider had escaped. On the fourth day, hanging from wall to water pipe was an exquisite web with a fat spider perched right in the center. What excitement! So many things on the journey happen spontaneously. The *real* curriculum often happens while you're busy planning something else!

Our discarded Halloween pumpkin became Mousekin's wonderful golden winter house.

DEMONSTRATION

Demonstration is another useful technique for bringing a story to life.

Modeling literacy activities in real-life settings is important for children to observe and experience.

Writing grocery lists, looking up phone numbers, reading the morning paper, sharing conversations at meal time, corresponding with families, and reading directions out loud are all fascinating to young children when they are themselves involved in the process. To involve children, for example, you might explain what you're doing, ask children if they want to add anything to a list, dictate thank-you notes, have them watch you write something out, listen to you read directions, and observe how you follow those directions. Feeling a part of what adults are doing and having the child's beginning literacy attempts at imitation accepted and celebrated are an important accompaniment to our demonstrations.

You can involve others in demonstrations as well: Whenever you have parents, grandparents, community helpers, directors, principals, or siblings coming to visit, ask them to bring a children's book (preferably something they remember from their own childhood) to read to the class. An alternative to reading might be to have visitors tell a story about a special experience from their childhood. These stories could be taped, then typed for a class scrapbook on visitors' stories. The following are a few ideas for modeling and demonstrating with young children.

Recipe Reading

Reading the recipe aloud from a book and picture coding a recipe for children are both valuable literacy experiences. It takes a conscious effort to use the moment to expose and explore the written words or symbols. It is also an opportunity to use the symbols and words in the languages represented in the class. Small group cooking experiences can demonstrate to the children that the words being read have immediate meaning and help them begin to make those important connections.

Imitation

We know we've modeled interesting things when children imitate what we've done. A parent noticed that her young son was watching intently as she put stick-on notes in her textbook while studying for an exam. When the phone rang, she left her book and pad on the couch. Her son took up where she left off and plastered her book with stick-ons and scribbled notes. When she returned, he told her he had written some notes for her. They were greatly appreciated, as you can imagine.

Real Connections

There is a wonderful poem by David McCord (1980) called "Pickety Fence." He has so beautifully described in words what the fence sounds like when a stick is run along its surface. One day while out on the playground, the teacher ran a stick along the fence saying: "pickety fence, pickety fence, give it a lick it's a lickety fence . . . lickety, lick, lickety, lick . . . " The children delighted in joining in the activity and creating their own "sound" words. When they went in for group time and the teacher read the poem, one lad picked up on the real-life connection: "Hey, that's just what our fence said!" A simple illustration, but demonstrations can be subtly powerful.

Model Reading

In one preschool, the teacher not only has her children look at books independently before snack time, she also lies down on the floor and reads her adult book beside them. This is a strong message that reading is important. It takes advance planning and organization if you have another transition coming (e.g., snack time). The transition from reading to snacking will be less hairy if everything is ready to "wheel out" when the children are finished with their silent reading.

EXPECTATION

Children's expectations are another important element in learning to read.

As adults we communicate in very subtle ways what we expect children to learn. Through children's engagement with the literacy journey, we want them to try, enjoy, succeed, risk without fear of failure, and expect that their attempts will be accepted, supported, and when appropriate, celebrated.

The expectation and trust of the significant people in their lives have a powerful effect on what children can achieve. An open, accepting atmosphere creates a healthy climate in which all children have the potential to grow. It is especially important, however, for the growth of our children with disabilities. If children can expect, within reason, that their setting will be consistent, supportive of their attempts, foster cooperative learning, and nourish their interests, then they'll engage with more confidence and success in the process of real learning. Cambourne (1988) states that: "the expectations of those to whom the learners are bonded are powerful coercers of behavior . . . and that we are more likely to become engaged with those people we regard as significant and who hold high expectations for us." Gaining an understanding of our own expectations for each child and observing each child's behaviors will give us valuable clues for the development of our literacy journey. For example:

Peer Significance

Not only do adults have a strong influence in the area of expectations, but the power of the peer relationship also must be held in high regard. A child who could not communicate verbally was delighted when her friend plopped a hat on her head, held her hand, and pranced off with her as another one of the monkeys in

Caps for Sale. It was just expected that she'd go along in the replay—and she eventually did, with the insistent hand grasp of her buddy. She knew the story and just what to do, but was reluctant to join until her peer led her into the experience.

Finding a Way to Participate

One young boy who was hearing impaired excitedly tried to "tell" his teacher something he wanted to share. No matter how he struggled to verbally or gesturally explain his news, no one could understand what he was trying to say. In frustration, he grabbed a black crayon and drew squiggles all over a piece of paper like this:

The teacher guessed: "Let's see. Is it streamers? worms? string?" Someone tried: "Snakes?" Brandon's eyes danced and both thumbs went up as a sign of success! At the time, Indiana Jones was a big hero for some children. We assume that he had probably seen the movie *Raiders of the Lost Ark* over the weekend and was showing us the scary snake pit. He beamed and shook his head up and down with gusto when we asked him if indeed he had seen the movie. It was so important for him to communicate what was meaningful in his life. He wanted to engage us in sharing "the story" in the only way he had available. When his expectation that we could understand his verbal attempts failed, he had the motivation and confidence to draw his communication. It was the first time he realized he could actually convey meaning through his artwork! His mother later revealed that she had been drawing stick figures for him a few times when he didn't seem to understand her explanations. It was an interesting exploration of demonstration and expectation for all of us.

Deeper Understanding

Returning to favorite books and story-related materials should give children a richer knowledge of the story, its sequence, characters, and other essential components. Stories provide a testing ground for children at all developmental levels to "try on" and play with various ways to absorb and experiment with ideas, concepts, and personal meaning in literature and with other forms of literacy. For adults and children, retelling a story in the journey process involves variations using flannel boards, magnetic boards, shadow puppets, big books, miniature worlds, music, and any other means that encourage children's interest and engagement. It is therefore essential to supply the story replay materials so children can choose their medium. It is a legitimate expectation that the teacher will provide for these choices with careful consideration to the environment, the provision of resources, and children's varying abilities.

What Do Adults Expect?

John Dewey said that learning is a representation of experience. Put another way, it is "re-presenting" things in such a way that children at all developmental levels have a way to find meaning in their experiences.

Have you ever wondered if children really make sense out of some of the rhymes or story experiences we present? Are we assuming or expecting that they have found their own way to interpret or represent meaning? Children are so accepting and go right along with our rub-a-dub dubs, trip traps, and hey diddle diddles. Many of us who have been doing this for years have just enjoyed sharing the

"Reading" to a captive audience: Stories provide a testing ground for children to play with various ways to absorb and experiment with ideas, concepts, and personal meaning.

rhythm of these words and have never really stopped to think how a child may be conceptualizing such ditties. Two very special teachers who have been developing unique journeys with storybooks for a number of years set out to explore how one might have fun with presenting nudges around these whimsical phrases. While telling "The Three Billy Goats Gruff" one morning, Marillyn wondered if the children thought that maybe the three billys made the trip trap, trip trap sounds from their mouths. Most children are well-versed in cows mooing and pigs oinking, but few seem to know what goats say. Armed with heavy hiking boots, Marillyn talked about the noises that feet make with shoes on, and without shoes. She explained that we wear shoes, but billy goats do not need to; they have hooves. She slid thimbles on her fingers to demonstrate a hoof-like concept and told the finger puppet version so they could hear the 'trip trap' on the table top. When the children acted out the story, they used coconut halves to sound like the trip trap hooves on the bridge. The special moment, however, was when we had a real billy goat visit and we heard his hooves on our plank bridge and also his "blah" when he protested being tied up outside. Re-presenting the information in such a way helps children to conceptualize the meaning in many different ways.

An entirely different approach for *Hey Diddle Diddle* was done by Dennis, who forever enjoys playing with ideas and exploring and nudging children's creative thinking. One day while doing the nursery rhyme: "Hey diddle diddle . . . " he asked the children: "What ever is a diddle?" After offering many contributions, the group came up with a small piece of wood as the configuration of a diddle. Wood scraps were gathered and from there they were off on a very original representation of diddles: They painted diddles, made diddle people, diddle roads, and diddle towns. The project was open to anyone and the extensions grew from just one simple creative nudge. It was spontaneous, contagious, and such a unique way to concretely represent nonsense!

RESPONSIBILITY

Children need to learn to take responsibility for becoming more literate.

Brian Cambourne speaks about the importance of children becoming responsible for their own learning. Many of us share this belief and know that it takes patience and a partnership among teachers, parents, and children to actualize that belief successfully.

In today's world of hurry, hassle, and very little time at home for many families, the child care centers and the public school classrooms are assuming a larger role in the development of a child's sense of responsibility. Teachers who have taught for many years say that families provided much more support in this area in the past. Unfortunately, today's reality is that many teachers feel they are shouldering so much of this responsibility alone.

More than ever, parents and teachers must form a partnership that supports the education of all children. With larger classrooms, more diverse populations, and meager budgets, our strength will only come from everyone taking a role, no matter how small, in educating our youngest offspring.

The following is a brief look at the role each of us can play in supporting a responsible pursuit of literacy in the lives of children.

Teacher's Role

Teachers can foster the development of responsibility in a number of ways:

- Observe and discover the interests, learning styles, and pace of individual children.
- Trust that children can find their way and make sound decisions about their learning if the physical and psychological environment support that end.
- Help children to focus their attention, engage, and reflect on their own progress.
- Create individual and group options and choices about learning with guidance and affirmation.
- Know the school and community resources available for extending child and family learning.
- Welcome partnerships with parents and provide resources and pertinent information about development.
- Plan opportunities for children to take more responsibility for their own learning individually and in groups.
- Empower children to risk, explore, succeed, and safely fail.
- Be open to explore other avenues of literacy with the family if English is not the family's first language, if a parent is not literate, or if other issues must be considered.

Parents' Role

The parents' role is not unlike that of the teacher's; their mutual influence will have long-term ramifications on literacy learning. Some examples of parents' contributions are:

- Modeling literacy behavior.
- Providing safe, interesting, and enriching experiences.

- Setting genuine standards around expectations and responsibilities that family members will assume.
- Following through on those expectations and responsibilities.
- Being a sounding board and advocate for the child's efforts.
- Celebrating a child's genuine attempts.
- Maintaining open lines of communication with the school.
- Listening carefully to what a child is attempting to explain/say.
- Limiting the use of television and viewing programs together as a source of conversation, shared interest, and feedback.
- Reading, singing, and/or storytelling as a daily ritual.

Some Ideas to Support Parent Efforts

For parents to enter into a partnership with a teacher, they need to understand the program and trust and value the teacher. The reverse of this is also essential: Teachers must understand the child in the context of the family and trust and value the parents. The teacher is the one who most often needs to initiate the first move, since many parents are reluctant to "interfere." Here are some suggestions to support this effort in the area of literacy:

- Create a lending library and have tapes of stories made up in the family's first language as well as in English to accompany the books.
- Lend out videos of the classic stories so that parents and children can watch them together.
- Develop and lend out simple miniature worlds, puppets, flannel boards, and dramatic play props to encourage parents and/or siblings to playact the stories together.

Families gather at an evening workshop to make their own story props for their children.

Fathers came to school one evening to go through a storybook journey with the Muffin Munchers. This is a captured moment of open choice time.

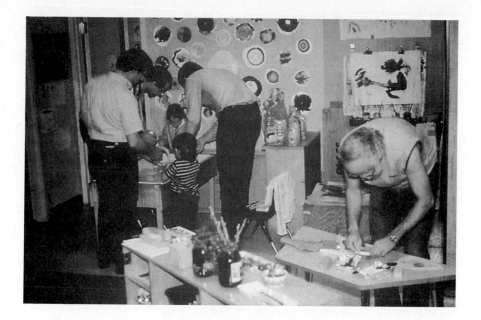

- Share incidently and in writing the benefits of a daily exposure to literature with those bonded to the child. Sharing the experience as a family with wonder, questions, dramatic play extensions, and discussions will build solid literacy foundations that will make the parents' efforts worth every moment!
- Encourage the public library to have story hour for families in a variety of languages.
- Hold an evening or weekend workshop in which families can make their own props for stories out of trash-to-treasure items, either for or with children.

The Child's Role

For children to take responsibility and make personal decisions, they must feel safe and supported in doing so. The important adults in their lives need to balance how much they assist children's performance and how and when they expect them to take on the responsibility to perform independently. A child's first steps toward this effort and those that follow take an understanding of child development and a commitment not only from school, but also from school and home together.

In literacy development, a child can only move toward responsible choices if those choices are made available. If we look at building foundations for literacy, then almost everything provided in a carefully planned environment has potential ingredients: the negative/positive space of puzzles; drawing, scribbling, writing, painting, spelling attempts; the kind of books available to children; the planning and placement of the blocks on the shelf and how the child places the blocks while building with them; the problem solving and creative thinking involved in long-term projects; and the endless array of other materials and personal interactions.

It is really important to connect the young child's role with that of the teacher and parent. Young children need the adults in their lives to model responsibility and to be responsible. Literacy exposure and enjoyment are a critical part of that responsibility. If parents and teachers enrich the soil around the "seedlings" in their charge and observe and tend to the important things, children will eventually become responsible for themselves.

USE

Materials are a useful way to supplement the storybook journey.

Children should have every possible opportunity to make choices that allow them comfort level and expertise with stories and other forms of literacy. This can be done using a pace and variety of materials that complement the individual child's style of learning.

Ways to enhance literacy exposure and experiences will be discussed in the other chapters and in various forms in this chapter. The immersion section and the chapter on materials spell out some of the possible choices for a child to practice, use, remember, transform, and approximate with stories. In addition to what has been discussed previously, the stories themselves become a springboard for the child's unique versions of these stories and experimentation with some original attempts at using words to create their very own stories.

Exposure to Story Language

Many adults living and working with young children find meaningful ways to include and use story language in their story times. They talk about the title, the author, the illustrator; the themes, plot, story sequence, and characters; the beginning, middle, and end; and the roles the characters take in the development of the tale. Being able to talk about the plot and characters is a valuable skill to acquire. Sharing this information in an informal way at an early age builds confidence for the later years, when it is expected behavior.

Sendak, Dr. Seuss, Shel Silverstein, and many others have written a wide variety of stories and poems that expose children to new words, nonsense terms, rich vocabulary, rhythmic phrases, and unique ideas. This exposure offers a delightful experience for building an awareness of and playful appreciation for the use of words and language.

Real-Life Experiences

Connecting, using, and associating stories with the child's real-life experiences generates new meaning. Selecting and using stories that relate to what is relevant in the young child's world (baby-sitters, parents, grandparents, behaviors, feelings, sports, nature, pets, siblings, friendships, daily routines, school, child care) are often an important beginning "look" at literacy. Display books on those subjects prominently so that they encourage children to become engaged on their own or to want to have them read aloud.

Individual Comfort Levels in the Use of Stories

Certain stories seem to cast a spell and eventually absorb all children in the replay. "The Three Billy Goats Gruff" has been such a story over the years. It has almost universal appeal even though the children's ability to reenact the details is distinctly individualistic. Within one integrated classroom there were three different retellings. Each child found a way to use and internalize the story at his own developmental level and capability. Peter was one little fellow who became uneasy at the group time reenactment of "The Three Billy Goats Gruff." He wanted to join in but appeared to be uncertain about crossing the shaky plank bridge as the littlest goat. After several start-up attempts, he decided to go through the "water" instead. The teacher immediately switched from "trip trap" to "splish splash," much to the delight of this little billy goat. The child sensed that his individual pace and style were not only accepted, but respected, and that the teacher's sensitive intervention was a shared understanding. He eventually went on to cross the plank with great confidence. He appeared to need to practice when no one was looking and perhaps to take more time to feel comfortable in this setting.

In another section of the room, Zachery was meticulously placing the flannel troll under the bridge and then the three billy goats in order across the flannel board. He never uttered a word, but went through all of the motions in perfect sequence as each billy separately went across the bridge, from small to large, with the troll interrupting each crossing. It was like watching a silent movie. When he was finished, he carefully placed each piece back in the folder, again in order, and with the troll jumping out every time a billy goat was placed inside. When the task was completed he said: "The end" and closed the folder, tucked it back on the shelf, and went off with his hands in his pockets. He had a clear knowledge of the sequence and the beginning, the middle, and the end. It was a vignette that was significant for our observation of Zack's nonverbal comprehension.

Meanwhile, Matthew worked for two days on constructing a bridge out of wood scraps, a troll with red hair, and selecting three different size jar lids to represent the Billys. He retold the story with different voices for the Billy Goats and a growly troll reenactment with grimacing facial expression and all the actions. He gathered quite a crowd as he got into the drama of his replay. He also had rapt attention at home, while telling it to his little brother. In the same classroom, all three children found a way to use what was available in the room to represent and re-present what was meaningful and appropriate for them regardless of their developmental capabilities. Jean Piaget (1967) has helped us to see the significance in diversity . . . "to understand is to discover or reconstruct by rediscovery. Such conditions must be complied with if in the future individuals are to be formed who are capable of production and creativity and not simply repetition!"

APPROXIMATION

Children's approximation of the stories they read is another essential element in literacy learning.

Every miniature world, writing setup, paint easel, and block shape is a potential support for a child's attempt to approximate a story, an event, or a place in their real or imagined world. Reading, writing, singing, and communicating also give young children endless chances to experiment, invent, practice, and master what will be critical lifelong skills.

Celebrating the approximations as children try out various possibilities encourages them to grow and extend their abilities. The keen observer will capture many incidents of children going about their daily tasks creating a semblance of what they have seen, experienced, listened to, or interpreted in their own unique fashion. We can learn so much from their associations, connections, and misconceptions.

Meaningful Beginnings

One child had worked for a good part of the day on a very elaborate block structure. When it was time to clean up, he couldn't bear to tear it down. No doubt many of you have experienced this in your classroom. The custodian liked the floor cleared at night so he could vacuum with ease and the teacher was trying to weigh the needs of both parties. She finally suggested that maybe Ben could write a note to the custodian. This was Ben's approximation: "PDTNKDMB." He asked the teacher to come over so that he could read it to her and she could help him tape the note on the structure. He "read" it to her and helped tape the note onto the structure. It read: *Please don't knock down my blocks!*

Special Events

Setting up environments with diverse ways of retelling stories allows children to find the medium that is most comfortable for their beginning attempts. Teachers can also encourage this by modeling the use of puppets, pine cone Billy Goats Gruff, or other props to use for storytelling. Setting up "special events" to encourage and document story retelling or approximations is also helpful. For example, one teacher set up a section of the room to be a pretend bedroom. She told the children that she was going to bed and one at a time they could come and tuck her in and tell her a good-night story. A camcorder captured all of the children's stories, which ranged from imaginative, made-up stories to approximations of their favorites. Aaron, a young lad with Down's syndrome, did a delightful thing: He came into the room and saw the teacher "in bed." He hugged her good-night and she asked him to tell her a story. He started to tell the three bears: "Mama bear, baby bear, papa bear." He looked at the teacher, pointed a finger at her and said: "Out bed!" He said that three times, stomped his feet, paused and yelled: "Out bed!" When the teacher reacted to his yelling by pulling the covers up to her nose as if frightened, Aaron said: "I'll huff, puff . . . blow bed down." None of us could contain ourselves when we looked at the tape together—this was indeed a precious and unique approximation to celebrate! (If you can't get papa bear to get out of bed—then switch to the lines of the big bad wolf and huff, puff him out of bed!)

A Child's Approximation and the Teacher's Extension

The repetition, meaningful imitations, turn taking, and contagious quality of the stories tend to eventually draw all children into the dramatic replays during the course of their open choice and/or group times. In the fall of his school "career," three-year-old Johnny had only one word in his vocabulary that he used with confidence: "Hey!" Hey meant everything from "Pay attention to me" to "Hey . . . he took my bike, I want more juice, or get out of my way!" When the class was playing out the story of "The Three Billy Goats Gruff" one day, Johnny wanted to be the troll. He and the teacher hid under the bridge. When Johnny heard the billys coming, he flew out from his hiding place yelling "HEY." What power Johnny felt as the goats stopped dead in their tracks on his one-word command. The teacher extended his efforts by using his "Hey" and then adding " . . . who's that crossing over my bridge?" He was delighted and the children saw him as an equal participant in the role play. Both Johnny and his peers knew the story so well that Johnny's body movements and "hey" approximation of the troll's command were not only understood, but accepted. The teacher's sensitive use of Johnny's "hey" and extension to the words the children knew best supported Johnny's efforts and legitimized his role in the play.

RESPONSE/FEEDBACK

Feedback is an important part of literacy learning.

All of us look to those we respect for feedback. It is an important part of our growth process and that of children. The tenor and intent of the feedback can have an impact on how children will respond in the future. Their attempts to become literate must be supported by our patient, knowledgeable, and constructive feedback.

All of us need both challenge and support in order to grow and learn. Young children need more of our "supportive" feedback in the beginning as they are just getting started on their own repertoire. After we know each child as a distinct individual, we will become more adept at offering individualized challenges, suggestions, questions, responses, and meaningful feedback.

Adult-to-Child Response

In these early years it will be particularly important to frame our responses to the child's beginning attempts at literacy in positive terms. A look, a tone of voice, and the choice of words can all be important elements of response to the sensitive child. If we want children to initiate ideas and be motivated to try out these ideas, we need to think about our method of feedback and the long-term development of a child's confidence to take risks in learning. Cambourne (1988) expresses it well: " . . . response must be relevant, appropriate, timely, readily available, nonthreatening, with no strings attached."

Child-to-Child Response

Another perspective on response is the child-to-child point of view. Children usually don't mince words when surveying the work of their peers and will exclaim in disgust: "What's that suppose to be?" or "*That's* a dog?" Sometimes this is followed by laughter, peer poking, and finger pointing. This is pretty tough feedback, but it's real.

How do we help children to be aware of the impact these comments have, especially if we are including children of all abilities in one classroom? Respecting each child and modeling the words and actions of caring are a beginning. However, children who tend to put others down are children who want time, attention, and positive responses themselves. As we see more and more families struggling to find time to be families, we realize the need for schools and centers to support children to respond responsibly and comfortably with each other. It is a vital part of our classroom learning.

Meaningful Involvement and Feedback

Research and years of experience have shown us that familiarity with the knowledge of stories, the variety of ways available to gain this information, and the time for reflection and repetition are the critical foundation on which children build their understanding. The culminating experience for a journey is often a reenactment of the story with the group. This is done through various combinations of adults or children or both. For us the critical point is personal, meaningful engagement and interaction at some level, the feeling of well-being and group camaraderie in the common knowledge of a story, and the sheer joy of being involved.

The story replay and mastering process also indicates how well children conceptualize the essence of the story and can integrate it at the various developmental levels.

How one measures involvement or balances the role of teacher and child in the replay process is very tricky. One must constantly ask: "Whose 'show' is this?" One teacher relayed the situation in which he found himself while reenacting "Jack and the Beanstalk." One day he and the children were very involved in the dramatic replay, sticking fairly close to the book version. When the teacher said: "And when the giant's wife opened the door . . . *who* was standing there?" Many voices yelled out "Jack," but one child appeared at the door in a green cape and pointed hat announcing he was "Peter Pan." Cut! Those of us who have taught for awhile know the thousands of instantaneous decisions one must make in the course of a teaching day. Again the question arises: "Whose show is this?" With various needs, abilities, and personality types to orchestrate, how does one continue the flow of the replay and incorporate the ingenious sidetracks that children are so capable of throwing our way? This little fellow in green not only wanted to visit the giant as Peter Pan, he wanted to change the story. Now we have his needs and the group needs to respond to and meet. There is not time to analyze the situation and there is no reference book with a solution for a story replay emergency. This is the essence of decision-making on your feet and risk-taking as you quickly decide to either support the child's wanting to lead or you try to reestablish control of the situation. There are no easy answers, but there are many questions we can discuss around the issues. In this case, "Peter" was willing to be "Jack" dressed up as Peter Pan and the story continued in the version the *group* wanted to tell. We all know that solutions are not always so simple. It would be very helpful to discuss this incident with the class team at the close of the day. Some of the possible issues that could be involved here are: How do you maintain interest, involvement, and flow while meeting the needs of various players? What options are available for addressing the issues with the children? When do you do this? What kind of feedback do your responses, subtle or not so subtle, model to the child and the group? There are no set answers, but an incident such as this opens up a wealth of opportunities to develop a cooperative approach to solving problems together and for reflecting on the effectiveness of the feedback.

Home-School Feedback Loop

One teacher in a cooperative preschool reported that a child arrived one Monday morning with the frightening news that: "A robber breaked into our house *late, late* last night and we all screamed and screamed." The other children were all ears, as you can imagine, and the play for the rest of the week centered around robbers. In observing their play, the teacher realized that part of the attraction was coming from the contagious nature of their fear and that they were never able to bring any of those fears to a resolution. The teacher looked for books that they might "journey with" that would be helpful, but nothing seemed appropriate. In this case, she turned to her greatest resource: the children. Over the following week they created their own book, *Things That Scare Us at Night*. Chapter 1 listed things that they fear: whistling wind, shadows, someone under their bed, break-ins, dogs barking at them, fire, weird sounds, waking up and thinking no one is home, and the like. Chapter 2 listed what to do or what they have done when frightened at night: "Call mom; bury your head under the covers; dial 911 and yell 'help,' and tell them where you live; pile up all your bears and hide behind them; get guns." The fears and the solutions varied as much as the children themselves; but what their "story" did was give the teacher a glimpse inside their feelings that she could respond to and discuss with them. They drew pictures to go along with their words and put it all together in a large book format. The teacher encouraged the children to take the book home as a way to let families know that four-year-old fears and worries are very real! A note from the teacher in the front of the book suggested that families may want to help their own children on a very personal level, to know what they can do to feel safe in their own homes. This feedback to the families is essential. Sometimes children's responses to trauma are delayed and the communication between home and school is a vital link to the child's emotional well-being.

Implementing the Journey

*O*nce upon a time there was a little boy whose engagement with the tale of Peter
Pan *became so powerful and significant to him that it set off the beginning ripples of this journey. The story of Dylan forms the bridge linking the philosophical
aspects of the journey process to its implementation with young children.*

Rod Hitchcock

*I*n a fairy tale the internal processes are externalized and become comprehensible as represented by the figures of the story and its events. . . . The realistic nature of these tales is an important device, because it makes obvious that the fairy tales' concern is not useful information about the external world, but the inner processes taking place in an individual.

~Bruno Bettelheim

The Journey Begins with a Child

D ylan stood in the doorway linking the inside and outside world of his center, a special school for preschoolers with developmental challenges. He observed from a distance and upon occasion, rode a bike around the macadam track—expressionless, without a sound, negotiating the world in a rigid, repetitive fashion with limited skills and motivation. He bristled when approached or encouraged to try something. He never spoke. He was three years old and deeply troubled. The depth of his childhood depression and failure to thrive were haunting to witness.

The center had two bus runs each day, and the small van we rode in became the extended classroom. It was an enclosed space for focused attention, much storytelling, reading, puppets, and window gazing with running commentary. Dylan was the first one on the bus each day. He always sat in the same front seat. This became a safe place for Dylan to ultimately be more willing to take risks. He started to talk in two or three word utterances, primarily about things he saw out of the bus window. He'd become noticeably frustrated as his ideas seemed to outrun his speech.

After months of being with us, Dylan gradually began to express himself more coherently and with more affect. He wanted to engage trusted adults in what he saw and began to cuddle up closer and closer to them while looking at books on the bus. In school he remained a solitary player and keen observer. One morning, upon entering the bus, Dylan discovered a Walt Disney version of *Peter Pan* that was a part of our permanent Bus Library. He went for that book daily after the first discovery, looking at every page in silent rapture. He carried it into the classroom one morning and asked to have it read over and over again by any adult who would read it to him. As time went on, he'd look at the book and label all the characters and selected events. We introduced other versions of the book and a simple record rendition of the story to add to his repertoire. He even enjoyed Mary Martin in the original recording of the Broadway musical production of *Peter Pan*. Other children were intermittently interested and took parts as we read the story on the bus; Dylan loved *always* being Peter Pan. Something was beginning to move Dylan. He was intensely motivated to master the story sequence and all the characters, although it was a story far more complex than we ever would have chosen for him.

With his gorgeous blue eyes, Dylan looked up at the teacher sitting close to him on the bus one day and said, "I dreamed I be Peter Pan last night!" For the first time, he had revealed something about his world beyond school, an abstract expression of his total preoccupation with the story. The teacher suggested they could play Peter Pan and asked Dylan what would be needed. He named everything—Wendy, a Wendy house, Michael, John, the Lost Boys, Captain Hook, Tinkerbell, and *Peter*!

Dylan now transformed the narrative to conform to his own story script with lots of flying and returning to a makeshift Wendy house in one corner of our play yard. One song Mary Martin sings ("Let's be quiet as a mouse and build a tiny little house for Wendy. Who's here to stay . . . a mother, a mother, at last we have a mother. . . . ") became very significant to Dylan. He liked us to sing it sometimes while he was "flying around." Dylan's mother was a very young single parent who was having a difficult time being a mom. The play around Wendy's house and the song about having a mother seemed to reflect some of Dylan's personal feelings and thoughts. We began to realize that Dylan was a "lost boy," and when he was playing Peter Pan, Wendy was a "mother" to him. Watching the freedom that flying allowed his body, and the momentary release from the tension and anger that was being carried by this little human being, was a moving sight for the team to observe.

Dylan's personality began to emerge through his identification with Peter and not growing up, outsmarting Captain Hook, the ability to "fly" and having a best friend, Tinkerbell! One day, Dylan, in a creative burst of symbolization, announced that his seat belt, in catching the afternoon sun, was Tinkerbell! It was instantly contagious. He sensed it, as all the children reflected their personal Tinkerbells on the bus ceiling. The world was responding to him, and he to it.

The environment and the adults provided the reality constancy for Dylan. He began to trust his world and sense himself in relation to others. It was a safe place and he had consistent, supportive adults on whom he could depend. He began to catch up in almost all areas of development. He was curious about everything and intent on listening to answers to his questions. He loved math concepts and reading street signs. He began to master frustration and to express deep feelings verbally. The adults continued to accept his onlooker style of quiet assimilation before he could join in the play or actively participate in a theme. They supported and extended his efforts so that he could become an active participant when he knew the theme. Peter showed up now and then in his thoughts, art, play, and sensory integration therapy. Lying prone on the net swing and trapeze during his sessions with the occupational therapist provided just the props he needed to fly like Peter. He eventually went on to try everything with the group—as Dylan! With guidance from the staff at school, Dylan and his mother were beginning to find a way to relate to each other. Books played a significant role by providing them with a means to build a new relationship and the vehicle for meaningful communication.

In his final months at the child-care center, Dylan could even initiate and direct socio-dramatic play. Themes varied between superheroes and storybook characters; they encompassed all his worlds. This little boy's struggle and eventual growth touched us all deeply. Dylan's total involvement with Peter Pan encompassed all areas of his development and opened a window on life for him that allowed a connectedness with the rest of the world. Its personal meaning to this little boy was almost beyond our comprehension. He taught us that stories hold a significant place in building a curriculum with young children at all stages of the developmental spectrum! It inspired us to look carefully at the significance of storybooks and their potential power in the lives of other children.

Certain conditions were necessary for Dylan to trust and grow with a fading dependence on Peter Pan. The powerful human relationships he shared, the careful development of the physical and psychological environment, the thoughtful selection and organization of materials, the communication between home and school, and a keen understanding of development and the role of play were all vital parts of the process. Part II will share all of these aspects in separate chapters integrating the philosophy throughout in a spirit that allows children to lead the way and adults to creatively extend children's interests.

A house that smiles,
props which invite,
and space which allows.

~Fritz Redl

Along the Road

Environments to Enhance Emerging Literacy

This chapter will

Discuss the physical and psychological atmosphere in a setting for young children by
- *Exploring the creation of inside spaces*
- *Defining child-created spaces*
- *Encouraging development of inclusive and private places*
- *Providing for the developmental range*
- *Sharing ideas about using outdoor spaces for literacy props*

THE PHYSICAL AND PSYCHOLOGICAL ATMOSPHERE

We've hiked quite a long way now on a rather philosophical route. Perhaps this would be a good time for us to stop and share some of the important issues in developing both the physical space and the psychological climate in our environments for young children. This stopover also allows us time to "check" our backpacks. This is important because the environment offers tangible evidence of the match between our philosophical grounding and how we develop our spaces.

The importance of creating an environment that welcomes and invites children to come learn with their own style and pace is essential to the success of the storybook journey. Equally important is a space that invites and allows children to function safely and with much freedom and choice to investigate, discover, experience, transform, test, risk, experiment, succeed, fail without fear, and become as intensely involved with what is meaningful and engaging to them as time and schedules allow. The organization of this space for young children functions best when it makes sense to all who live there. If it is carefully developed, the environment can actually be viewed as a spacial prop for independent and shared learning. It can support and strengthen the activities that take place there. Architecturally and as an accommodation for learning, the environment can offer pathways to all who live there for a novel way to assimilate their world.

"Putting together environments is really a way of 'seeing' . . . a way of looking at a situation . . . determining what might be done and acting on your feelings about it" (Ashby, 1973). It's a way of cultivating what we value for children and what we want to foster in our settings. Sound environments not only emanate from the development of physical spaces for learning through play, but also depend upon the psychological climate in which children and adults learn to live together. They are inseparable components and vital if we believe that children learn best when they are emotionally comfortable, actively engaged with their surroundings, and beginning to feel socially connected.

Let's begin by entering our environment through a child's eyes; not only how it looks to the child, but also how it might feel. It helps to start by getting down on our knees, since that is the approximate viewpoint of a young child and will give us quite a different perspective as an adult. By placing ourselves at the child's eye level, we quickly become aware that the children who navigate this space are really nose to nose with the backs of chairs, table legs, clutter on shelves, the bottoms of pictures, and adult knees. If we return now to our usual stance as adults, we scan over most of this and our eyes tend to focus on the surrounding walls and table tops. Quite a different view, isn't it? We must constantly remember the setup needs to make sense to the children. How will they see it, experience it, and use it?

In the busy pace of our lives with young children it is sometimes hard to stop long enough to observe and reflect on what is really happening in our space. Take a moment. It is very important to look at the subtle or not-so-subtle messages the environment might be conveying to the children and their families as they enter this setting each day. Creating an atmosphere that matches our philosophy of child development means paying attention not only to the physical elements and configuration of space, but also to the psychological tone of warmth and caring that we wish to exchange. Thelma Harms (1979) has said that the way people treat children is as real a part of the environment as the materials or the shelves or the space provided for block building. The adults' tone of voice, walk, facial expressions, and stance all have an impact.

Children are being exposed to a world of sensory overload everywhere they go today, and many children have trouble regulating this bombardment. For children to function and learn at their own level of comfort, the adults in their lives must consciously observe and monitor the use of the space, the atmosphere, and the tone in the room, along with the feelings of the children and adults themselves.

The monitoring might include a diagnostic scanning of everything that could enhance the capacity for an optimal environment of rich learning and emotional and physical comfort. We could call such scanning using our common "senses": what do we see, hear, smell, and feel in the environment and what effect it might be having on those who spend their day there. The physical and psychological atmosphere in an environment is basically affected by all that is happening in that space: human relationships, size of the room, number of children and adults, safety and appropriateness of the equipment, ventilation, heat, lighting, noise level, colors, surfaces, what and how things are hanging on the walls, organization, cleanliness, accessibility of materials, defined areas, pathways, and the variety of spatial levels. Each of these variables can enhance or detract from the overall atmosphere. Regulating temperature and ventilation is imperative to a healthy body and, for almost all children, the need for private spaces and soft pillows is equally imperative to a healthy soul. Children react to their environment with every part of their being, and they deserve to have our careful attention to providing the most appropriate surroundings for their continuous growth. Humans and the storybook journey thrive in such an environment.

Defining Spaces Inside

Children's own needs and interests are supported or devalued by what a given setting provides. Together spaces and private places, noisy and quiet, light and dark, stark and cluttered, simple and complex, high and low level variations, hard and soft, flexible and fixed, open and enclosed, wet and dry are all part of the varied choices available. How these spaces are arranged communicates expectations about how they are to be used. Adult modeling is also helpful in setting up expectations of how an area might be experienced. For example: reading or telling stories in the quiet spaces or stretching out on the floor to observe the baby mice together; setting up the water table and paints in the wet area; cooking and using Playdough in the areas that are easiest to clean up and being noisy and active in the larger spaces that allow for freedom of movement.

Noisy and Quiet

Victor Lowenfeld (1935) had a wonderful way of saying how important provision for noise is in an environment for young children: "Noise is necessary, movement is necessary, and to be healthy these must be allowed to be exactly what they are— shapeless explosions of an over-plus of energy." Noise *is* a necessary part of young children's lives and a very important element to be carefully considered in developing spaces for young children. The paramount thing to remember is to set up noisy sections in the more active part of the room (blocks, trucks, woodworking, large motor activities). It is also wise to give this area some elbow room for the use of large equipment and movement. It is important to have a flexible space for setting up gross motor equipment and activities. Equally important is the creation of quiet spaces. Enclosed areas for individual or small group story replays with flannel or magnetic boards, puppets, miniature worlds, listening tapes, and the like are very satisfying and conducive to a concentrated pursuit of storytelling or imaginative daydreaming. Comfortable places to curl up, stretch out, or sink into are befitting of such a quiet, reflective space. One classroom I visited used only household lamps and natural light throughout the room. The effect was a cozy, soft, homelike setting. It was especially enticing in the book nook. Many children need to pull out from the pace of an ongoing crowd. They need idle time for private thoughts and wondering. Pillows around a fish tank or ant village can often encourage or legitimize their efforts to calm themselves or just retreat for awhile. It often has the same effect as a window seat for those of us who have such a retreat from which to quietly survey the world.

Children's Input

One teacher of four- and five-year-olds in a child-care center had become quite concerned about the use of space and materials in his classroom. He tried a very dramatic remedy. He removed everything from the room and covered it with sheets out in the hall. When the children arrived the next day, the teacher greeted them in a totally empty room. You can imagine the children's surprise. After the initial shock and questions, the teacher asked the children to think about what they wanted to have back in the room. Books topped the list for the first order! (We were naturally thrilled to hear about that.) Blocks, a few chairs, and tables were brought back into the room as the children began to think about what they needed to create their environment. Perhaps the critical point in what transpired in this situation was that the children played a pivotal role in decision-making about their space. They had to think about and discuss each new suggestion and their requests were respected and implemented. There was focused attention on equipment, materials, spatial arrangement, and what was important for all who "lived" in this room. A renewed sense of ownership in the classroom, a commitment to a certain order, and a great opportunity to throw out junk or store the unused prevailed.

Not everyone would want to stage such an event or take such a risk, but this task has some elements that you might want to ponder. Children tell us, by their behavior in or avoidance of a certain area in the room, which spaces need analysis by the team and/or discussion with the children. When spaces are crowded, misused, or inspire children to begin to use each other as equipment, we need to look carefully at the needs of the children, the arrangement of the physical space, and the equipment. Start with one area in your room that is a problem for whatever reason. Look to your parents, team, director, supervisor, or the like as a resource. Perhaps one of the above could observe the area and note what is going on or not going on in that space. Be certain to have the children discuss this with you also. From there you can begin to understand what changes you need to make. We have found that many times just switching the placement of centers—trading the dramatic play area with the book nook, for example—opens up a whole new interest. Of course, in the move you clean up, reorganize, add a few novel touches, and thereby renew interest. It's like having a new coat of paint in your kitchen!

One year, when we were doing the story of *Molly Moves Out*, a few of the children thought it would be fun to "act it out" and move all the household paraphernalia from the dramatic play area. They lined up the wooden trucks and trailers and worked so hard to lift the play stove, refrigerator, sink, and cupboard up onto the "moving vans." The morning was a flurry of endless movement and, I might add, chaos. For the involved group it was truly a case of relishing the process with no idea of any end product or logical plan of furniture arrangement. They had such fun balancing the equipment and problem-solving how to keep it on the trailers

Flexible spaces become marvelous places for children to create their own story reenactments.

while they were moving, then how to get it off when they stopped. The adults, however, had to finally call a meeting of all "van drivers" to help them develop a plan as the equipment was being delivered to all different parts of the room and distressing the would-be homemakers. It was fascinating to watch them gain a sense of the environmental layout. They had gotten so caught up in the excitement of the moving process that they lost track of where they were moving or why. During our discussion, we realized that they used the space we had created well and knew what happened and where, but when they started changing it, they really didn't have a sense of putting all the household stuff back as a unified package. Though it was not the intention, the outcome really seemed to give the movers a much better sense of how and why each activity center was set up. The learning that took place for all of us was well worth the temporary upheaval.

Spaces That Become Their Places

All of us like to know we have a place to put those things that are special to us—a place that we trust to be used only by us and to hold things safely until we go home again. Children need those places, too, and they learn quickly to respect not only theirs, but others': the bin with their name, the cubby with their photo, the shoe box with their sticker. As adults we know that ownership in the room goes far beyond cubbies and bins. The exciting part is when children demonstrate that they know the *room* is really theirs. Boxes become hideouts and bedspreads are transformed into tent sides, creating marvelous spaces that become their places (see Figure 5–1). In England, many of the schools have walls that are alive with aesthetic displays of the children's artwork and a section of the room that is set up like a museum for looking at the clay or construction work of the children who live there. It values the uniqueness of each child's work and gives a very real sense of what is taking place in the classroom.

The environment also provides a valuable backdrop for the interactive life of the players on this journey. Flexible space becomes necessary for the frequently shifting themes and moods at this young age. Allowing for areas where children can re-create spaces for their own story reenactments is important. Multiple functioning furniture is also an asset as it provides support for their developing ideas.

In most programs across the country, funding limitations have necessitated and cultivated the most creative use of all available materials and equipment: An emptied shelf placed on the floor, so that the back is now the top, is a delightful mountain peak from which to survey the world, or a platform at just the right level for setting up small props for storytelling (see Figure 5–2). Tables can hold up sheets for impromptu houses for the three pigs or can be turned on their sides for puppet stages (see Figure 5–3).

A door jamb or two legs of an inverted table are ideal places to stretch a sheet and use that space as a puppet stage. Details can be painted or crayoned on the sheet for houses, barns, bridges, or whatever.

If adults encourage and model imaginative use of space and materials for spontaneous play, children will be more likely to do the same. One teacher in a child-care center threw a yellow bedspread over a dome climber, crawled underneath "the haystack," and started saying: "Little Boy Blue come blow your horn . . . " She had many little boy (and girl) blues who followed her in and later made haystacks of their own under chairs, tables, and then outside under the bushes. Children enjoy adapting spaces to their imaginative whims when the atmosphere promotes trust and empowers them to feel comfortable in their behavior.

Space Novelty and Variations

How often we hear child-care providers and educators lament that they wish they could build a loft or a pit into their environments. It's that longing for a change of levels, for some novel twist to keep the room interesting and challenging. Finances, shared spaces, roof lines, and other issues often make such variations in a room difficult. There are other ways to create novelty in a setting, however, such as building

Figure 5–1
An appliance box with a window and door cut out is a space that becomes a special place.

Figure 5–2
An emptied shelf placed on the
floor can become a platform for
storytelling with small props.

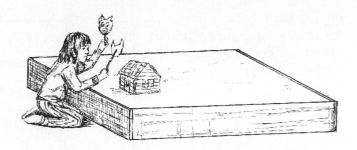

a series of platforms, filling a waterbed skin for the base of the book nook, bringing
in an old claw-footed bathtub and filling it with pillows for an interesting place to
relax in and observe from.

The creation of novel spaces can also be a very simple procedure of just rearranging existing areas or developing new props for enhancing the play schema of
the group. We've all set up doctor's offices, but have we included a waiting room
with magazines, chairs, and toys, and a receptionist area with phone, appointment
book, and lots of forms? With most parents in the work force, an office setup is a
real drawing card (see Figure 5–4). We took two big refrigerator boxes and opened
them up halfway to form a secluded space for an office. Cinder blocks and wooden
planks were set up inside to form the desk and spackling cans were spray painted to
become "office" chairs. Pencils, rulers, tape, scissors, telephone, an old adding
machine, a typewriter, and so on were rotated throughout the duration of this project so the children could try the tools of the trade.

Once, when we rearranged the housekeeping/dramatic play area because it was
not being used, we covered the back of the play refrigerator and sink with a huge
piece of cardboard from a washing machine crate. We left a space of about one and a
half feet between them and cut a door out of that piece. It brought great activity to
the area and the door was the *big* attraction. For the toddlers it was constant open-
ings and closings, for the three- and four-year-olds it was very purposeful, and for
the slightly older children it became a kind of saloon-door to burst through on their
way into the latest drama taking place in that space.

Children are encouraged to write at a number of places in the various activity
centers, but sometimes a special place is created in a quiet area of the room specifi-

Figure 5–3
A table turned on its side
becomes a puppet stage.

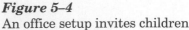
Figure 5–4
An office setup invites children to reenact their parents' workplace activities.

cally to invite writing, drawing, "chalk talks," journal entries, and making one's own books. Paper, staplers, food storage bags, a typewriter, and various other materials are available to support any interest in this endeavor. Changing the actual location of this little nook often rekindles the interest for some or catches the attention of a child who is just becoming engaged with the writing process. Books are distributed throughout the room for copying words if they are interested, and various extensions—envelopes, stick-up notes, stickers/stamps, small pads, and mailboxes—add a sense of purpose to beginning attempts at writing. So many stories refer to writing letters; a nook set up in this fashion encourages a very natural extension of their listening experience.

INCLUSION OF ALL CHILDREN

Environments can set the stage in various ways for active learning, social contact, dreaming, thinking, and exclusive retreating from the tempo, volume, and complexity of the larger setting. In developing environments for the inclusion of a diverse population, where storybooks and extended literacy experiences are an important focus, we may want to consider a number of issues, including developmental range, disabilities, physical challenges, and interaction with peers.

Providing for the Developmental Range

In every group of children, the way each child perceives and relates to the world will vary. In an integrated setting, these variations tend to be more dramatic, and the creation of an environment to meet the diverse needs—especially if space is limited—takes careful thought and planning. A focus on the representation of story environments and the re-presenting of stories creates many options for children to explore in play. Our observations of their behavior should tell us whether the environment and the materials speak to their needs and if these have personal meaning for them.

The child who needs predictable, realistic arrangements to reenact a story might benefit from a small house set up in the dramatic play area, a clear path through the woods from home to Grandma's house, and a basket of goodies for Red Riding Hood to take to grandmother. For other children, a pillow can serve as the bed, and they imagine the basket. While some children see everything in the room as a

For the child who needs predictable, realistic arrangements, for the reenactment of a story, there might be a small granny house for Red Riding Hood's grandmother in the dramatic play area.

stimulus for a possible prop, others are more comfortable having the perceptual space carefully and realistically prearranged. One setting can accommodate both types of behavior, with the children free to move between their own setups and those the adults provide. The optimum goal is to nudge children along to a more symbolic representation of the story props—but only as they are ready to explore that next possibility. Maintaining a balance between these two points of view is essential. Children who are developing and absorbing experiences in their own unique ways need to be able to go back and forth between the realistic environmental setups and those that are more abstract. They may do this by joining in, watching, or practicing in the security of the more private places they create at school. For some, the practice grounds are at home. Sharing what families observe in their home settings and what teachers observe in school is essential to evaluating the child's total experience.

Providing for Children with Disabilities

Accessibility to the building is mandatory for including all children. It is amazing how ramps get built once an organization decides to make the commitment. Parents, community agencies, and volunteer groups seem to come out of the woodwork if someone makes this a priority. Once the wheelchairs and special apparatus are in the room, then we need to study ways to arrange the space to accommodate the special equipment. More important, however, is to find creative ways to keep the equipment from separating the children from each other. If the group is on the floor and Joey is in a wheelchair, the levels further isolate Joey from the magic quality of being close to others at group time or at play. We can view this as a problem or a challenge. A brainstorming session involving parents, teachers, support staff (occupational therapists, speech pathologists, psychologists), and children can be an exciting way to tackle it. Unique ways to position children and ingenious plans for adapting equipment can materialize from just such a session. Yes, it takes time and work, but the results are well worth the investment of energy. In fact, all children deserve this kind of attention to their basic needs.

Offering Physical Challenges

Anita Olds (1982) has spent many years designing environments for young children. She addresses the critical role that physical facilities play in encouraging awareness and nourishing evolving capacities for assimilation and response. She also considers issues of developing the senses and providing opportunities for learning to move and moving to learn.

During the journey, we can seize opportunities to use story themes to enhance physical pursuits. Ropes become beanstalks, slides turn into drawbridges for a castle, and the jungle gym/climber is a tree for holding monkeys with caps as they flee from the sleeping peddler. In one setting, two old bean bag chairs and the filled inner skin of a waterbed were lined up as part of the course that the Tortoise and the Hare had to run in the race to the finish line. These different surfaces provided a unique balancing challenge and a source of good laughs to both the participants and the spectators. Another idea would be to set up three bridges over "the water" for "The Billy Goats Gruff." Children now have a choice: one bridge is made from a triangle climber, one from the foam packing materials used to ship computers, and the third from a narrow plank across two sawhorses. These extensions can add such fun to the story replay and provide physical challenges that delight the agile and entice those who need the experience.

Sensory activities can invite physical involvement in another form. "Mountains" of yellow shaving cream become haystacks for hiding Little Boy Blue. The outside world comes inside with snow in plastic bins and food coloring to add new dimensions to the retelling of *The Snowy Day*. In one setting, snow was piled high in the water table to represent the mountain so that The Little Engine That Could (and did) was able to climb up and over to the other side with its load of goodies. Burying one's arms in a tub filled with Jack's magic beans ("Jack and the Beanstalk"), tasting and smelling the three bears' porridge while it cooks (*Goldilocks and the Three Bears*), and dancing on mural paper with yellow and blue painted feet (*Little Blue and Little Yellow*) all add to the child's enjoyment of the related stories and provide an ever-changing means of expressing and understanding through the senses.

Fostering Interaction with Peers

Desks all in a row invite very different behavior than chairs arranged around small tables or pillows tucked in a corner. Encouraging children to be in touch with each other takes careful thought, not only in developing the environmental setups, but also in establishing the interpersonal atmosphere. Participation in reenacting a story encourages active interchange. Most stories have more than one character and thus entice more than one child to take on the various parts. A special enclosed area in the room for replay—puppet characters from a particular story or a miniature world setup, for example—creates a quiet, cozy atmosphere that can encourage more timid children. Some children will be drawn by the appeal of the props and thus be in contact with other children. Some will be drawn to a particular child, small group, or the adult who has plopped himself or herself in the area. Paying close attention to the gathering and development of the props, the presence of an observant/understanding adult, and the careful preparation of the space will often invite children to come play out a story together. The size of the space is important, too, as smaller spaces will dictate smaller numbers. The smaller the numbers, the more children will be encouraged to interact with each other. Watching and observ-

Snow was piled high in the water table to represent the mountains so the Little Engine That Could (and did) was able to climb up and over, bringing goodies to the other side.

ing is an important stage of learning for many children, especially children with special challenges. Watching is also a preliminary phase of peer contact and interaction.

For days, Billy would choose to drive his truck and park it by the small enclosed area where children would retell stories, either with the flannel board or the miniature world props. He'd lean over the low shelf and watch without a word. When the storytelling was over, he'd drive off. We never saw him participate in the process of retelling a story at school. One night, while falling off to sleep, he said: "Who on bridge?" "No!" "Eat up . . . " Billy had taken in so much and was practicing in the safety of his own room. With time, perhaps he would try a reenactment with his peers. Watching and practicing alone was for Billy an essential prerequisite to peer play and part of his own unique style of mastery.

USING SPACES OUTSIDE

Extending beyond the room—to explore meadows, ponds, rocks, and ditches; to ride on escalators as a corduroy bear; or to sit on walls all over town as Humpty Dumpty—is part of the environment. The outside world offers children the feel, sights, and smells of the world at different times of day and in different weather and seasons. Children know how to explore every inch. Greenman (1988) wrote: "The outdoors has weather and life, the vastness of the sky, the universe in the petals of a flower. But many programs, following the model of schools, have seen the very qualities that make the outdoors different as obstacles or annoying side effects. The openness is tightly constricted; weather provides a reason to stay in, and landscape and life are things to be eliminated. A playground, considered the primary, if not the only outdoor setting, performs the same function as a squirrel cage or a prison exercise yard—it is a place for emotional and physical release and a bit of free social interchange." Greenman has gathered the most comprehensive information on what children want to do outside. He suggests many alternative ideas to the standard playground. His chapter on outdoor learning is an excellent resource and well worth exploring.

The natural materials and spaces of the outside world provide unique opportunities for storytelling. When my children were little, they would gather dried grass, twigs, and assorted bricks to complete bush and tree root enclosures representing the houses of the three pigs or the witch's house for Hansel and Gretel. They used leaves to build nests, acorn tops became fairy cups, and pebbles from the nearby brook were the gold coins for the giant to count. At the beach, the sand and the shells provided endless extensions to their imaginative play. At one point in their lives they would dig huge sand pits to hunker down in, feeling warm and safe to spin their dreamy tales in these private enclosures.

Going to a wooded area or a place with high bushes or a few trees adds a new dimension to telling *Little Red Riding Hood* or "The Three Bears." One class went outside to the playground after reading "The Three Bears," and the children spontaneously started to play out the story. The bowls were various size pails, the sand was the porridge, the sandbox ledge served as the table, and the children created anything else they needed out of whatever they could find. When it came to beds, Fred just took a stick and made three different size circles on the ground and told everyone which bear would sleep in which "bed." No one questioned that those circles were indeed the beds.

When you go outside with your children now, try to find a wonderful place that might have any or all of the following: stones, pebbles, rocks, pine needles, leaves, horse chestnuts, acorns, pine cones, twigs, puddles, brook, bushes, bark, and other marvelous natural resources that you can discover. Tell the story of "The Three Little Pigs" or *The Three Billy Goats Gruff* using nature for your props. One day, when you do these stories (and so many others), invite the children to try the same process. The more we encourage using what is available instead of having to buy everything, the more we will instill the simple pleasures of creating and imagining. These natural props are also readily available when children play at home.

In closing this chapter on environments, I'd like to quote Judith Snow (1992), who spoke of environments in society as places "where dreams are heard, gifts are discovered, and interactions renewed." Certainly a slower tempo in life and more time to quietly and wisely observe what children are really doing would help us to discover their dreams, thoughts, interactions, and talents. Rushing to measure their endeavors by assessment yardsticks only compounds and limits our view of their imaginations, clever use of the environment, and their gifts.

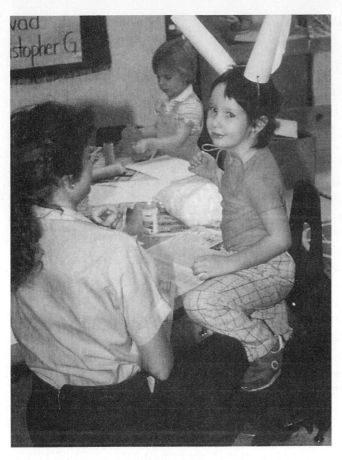

*T*he child's mode of being in the world is such that the world becomes an invitation. It is things in the beckoning world that invite the child, that awaken his curiosity, that invoke him to make sense of that multitude of experience lying beyond; in short to become, through his play, both an actor and a meaning maker.

~V. Suransky

Props for the Pilgrimage
Providing Materials for Exploration

This chapter will

- *Explore materials as a dynamic part of literacy and story development*
- *Advocate the use of recycled "trash" for prop building*
- *Suggest using natural and living things as materials for reenactment*
- *Share ideas on the use and creation of props for storytelling*
- *Recommend what to gather and suggest storage, display, and setup ideas*

SUPPORTING CHILDREN'S INTEREST

Materials can provide the tools for learning things which no one can teach. When open-ended materials such as water, sand, mud, clay, paper, blocks, and trash-to-treasure items are consistently available, children become engaged in acting upon them, organizing and changing them, exploring the possibilities and creating relationships among them. During this process they begin to gain an understanding of the properties of the materials with which they're working, the effect their actions have on the materials, and a new sense of wonder about themselves and the world around them.

The atmosphere in the room must be one of valuing and encouraging the child's attempt to use what is available in a variety of ways—testing, discovering, and integrating the various areas in the room by incorporating junk items into their ongoing play schema. Paper tubes can roll, unravel, and spin. They can form marble runways, car tunnels, silos, or binoculars. They can be lined up in sequence as the three bears. "When materials are not limited by boundary or form, they remain forever tools which a person uses differently as he grows to perceive the world differently" (Cohen, 1972).

Children are spontaneous researchers spurred on by their natural curiosity and attempts to make sense of their immediate world. One day while doing child-like "research," Matt discovered that by cutting three sides of a square space on a piece of paper he had created a "flipper." Held this way it became a garage door (see Figure 6–1). Held another way, it looked like a house door (see Figure 6–2). He went on to try it with cardboard, which worked better, and wood, which didn't work at all. Like Matt, other children want to push it, pull it, twist it, combine it, beat it, mix it, drag it, poke it, control it. They want to explore and manipulate real objects with their senses, their bodies, their minds, and their peers. They want to build on what they know, make decisions, and see results.

To support a child's interests and investigations, adults face the continuous challenge to establish the skills of

- observing
- experience priming

Figure 6–1
A piece of paper becomes a garage door.

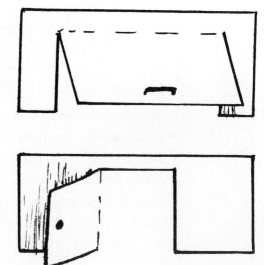

Figure 6–2
Held another way, the paper is a house door.

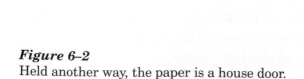

- tone setting
- material gathering
- creating
- constructive responding

For each of these skills our goal is to encourage and enhance children's extended opportunities for using materials to support their emergent literacy development and comprehension. While early childhood programs use materials to integrate *all* development, this chapter will focus mainly on the use of materials as they relate to story reenactment.

Observing

Dorothy Cohen (1978) used to say that children reveal themselves in special children's ways. Observing them carefully gives us clues and information to see them as they are and as they see themselves. During our observations we must be aware of what is significant to children. How often have "special" gifts wrapped in fancy paper been cast aside for what really had meaning: the *box* that contained the present? When we observe each child carefully as an individual and as part of a social context, we can begin to develop options and choices for individual children that will help them derive personal meaning from their experiences.

Brian was just such a child. After weeks of seeing him explore the preschool in his own way—touching things and pouring water for days, oblivious to the rest of the world—we set up a story replay with Brian in mind. We were doing the story of *Little Blue and Little Yellow* by Leo Lionni. We set up a plexiglass easel by the glass door so that the light would come through and give Brian a large transparent surface where he could explore the marvels of paint. He was totally engaged in the process of mixing the colors on the easel and in the paint cups. The light shown through in such a way that perhaps for the first time he really could wallow in the joy of "seeing" vivid colors with the very limited sight he has had since birth. Perhaps this is just what David Elkind (1987) meant when he said: "Education of children must be in keeping with their unique modes of learning." Our observations reveal those unique modes and help us make materials available to enhance children's experience and options.

Through our observations we begin to learn when to nudge children gently from the realistic materials in context to explore the more abstract. We can also see what challenges and what frustrates each child; who risks and who withdraws; who generates their own ideas and who needs support; who can approximate with confidence and who feels safer copying a peer or enticing an adult to do it for them. Our challenge is to move from observation to invitation. How do we set up materials so that children can explore and use their imaginations to the fullest?

Experience Priming

Careful attention to how we prepare or prime the environment both physically and psychologically is paramount to the journey. In our sincere attempt to teach, we can often rob children of their own discoveries. "We ignore what children have to learn and instead impose what we want to teach thus putting young children at risk for no purpose" (Elkind, 1987). It is therefore extremely important to prime the learning situation with experiences that children can relate to and explore over time. An example of this might be to bring in a caterpillar *before* reading *The Hungry Caterpillar* to the children. Watching the caterpillar devour all the dill in the jar each day

The light shone through in such a way that perhaps for the first time he could wallow in the joy of "seeing" vivid colors with his very limited sight.

before spinning its cocoon is a real-life experience that primes the children for a more whimsical adventure in story form.

We can also view priming as the preparation of the classroom for children's purposeful involvement in their own pursuit of knowledge and experience. Priming such an environment involves provision, organization, rotation, exploration, and preparation of materials.

Provision

Open-ended, hands-on materials must be accessible to children at all times. Children think best with all their senses and need to be able to see, touch, manipulate, and feel empowered to transform materials. Open-ended refers to materials that do not have a specific "correct" use and thus inspire the child's impact on them; sand, water, clay, paints, and mud are examples. They are multipurpose materials that allow random experimentation and a means to extend children's imaginations.

Organization

Organization of the materials must make sense to those using the space and encourage independent choices and clean up. The accessibility of such materials is paramount if children are to creatively pursue development of their own projects.

Rotation

Rotation of materials from storage space to classroom is another way to rekindle interest. If egg cartons, popsicle sticks, bottle caps, yarn, string, and other materials have been out for a long time and space doesn't allow for additions, only exchanges—rotate! Put different things in your bins, baskets, or boxes. Just changing "stuff" can prime curiosity and creativity. (Many have found that plastic see-through shoe boxes with lids work well for storage and display. The commercial, divided cardboard shelves with nine spaces for holding shoe boxes are excellent for both the classroom and the storage room. They organize and display the materials for easy viewing, accessibility, and rotation.

Exploration

In-depth exploration of one material at group time is another way to prime the creative flow. For example, if a child has brought in a bag of spools to add to the class collection of materials, hold up one spool at group time to brainstorm its uses. Children will feed off of each other's ideas for using it as a bubble blower, a bead for stringing, a ramp roller, wheels for a small car, a base for a doll house table, and more. This group priming before adding the spools to the project area of the room generates interest and ideas for later use. Writing the children's suggestions on a list with quick illustrations to assist in "reading" what they have shared is a helpful literacy nudge in the recycled project area.

Preparation

Preparation of thoughtful setups invites children to try, invent, discover, be challenged, and enjoy. It's a little like providing appetizers to unexpected guests. *It isn't always an issue of what we have or how much we have as it is how we vary the invitation* to try some of the same old stuff. Even carrots can seem very appealing by how we cut, display, and present them. It is what Chittenden said that teachers should do to arouse curiosity: introduce the novel in the context of the familiar. We want to encourage that "Gee, I'd like to try this!" feeling. Putting crayons out in various ways to inspire their use is a fun example of this process. We've tried arranging them for individual use in upturned egg cartons, tin adhesive bandage boxes, lying flat on meat trays, or in a pumpkin shell for Halloween. Presentation of materials can also prime the social aspects of learning. Putting all the crayons in one basket at the center of the table invites sharing, negotiation, and patience! It provides a marvelous opportunity to observe children's ability to navigate in the sometimes uncomfortable situation of having to wait for the color they want or deciding to grab the whole basket for themselves.

We have also done things like putting a story-related group of puppets in a closed box in the middle of the floor to stir up curiosity. Some just walk right around it, while others have to explore all its contents! Once we wore swim flippers on our feet to greet the children in the morning as a way of opening up discussion on the week's story of *Frog and Toad Together*. One classroom has a big stuffed bear that usually resides in the book nook. One day the staff put a yellow cowboy hat on his head and a scoop in his paw and moved him over to the water table that was filled with beans. He was a real drawing card for some very creative play with a pile of tired old beans. One teacher put a rope down the slide and pretended to be rescuing children from the "water." They were Timothy Turtle, Captain Hook, or just themselves. The teacher and a group of children would stand at the top of the sliding platform and hold the rope, while the child on the other end would climb up the slide using hand over hand on the rope. A simple idea, but fun and great for building upper-body strength. Another teacher used colored scarves on the slide. The children would lay the scarf down on the slide and zip to the bottom on a slippery flash of color. This takes time and inspiration, but the results are well worth the effort. It can eliminate some of the ho hum of setup and adds an element of fun to rearranging a given space or re-presenting materials in a variety of unique ways.

Tone Setting

Creating an atmosphere of acceptance balanced with challenges and time for experimental use of many materials helps children see their options. If they feel supported and valued for their efforts, ideas, and unique ways of interpreting the world, they are far more willing to independently master the mechanics and problem-solving skills for developing their story props with tape, scissors, paper, stapler, and brads. Frustration can build for some children as their mind's idea and the capabilities of their small hands don't always match. It is during such times that a patient, caring adult who can just slip in beside a child for a few minutes and "self-talk" the child through the problem is very helpful. For instance, one child was so frustrated with trying to figure out how to hold his sock puppet of Eeyore and sew the eyes on at the same time that he was about to throw it across the room. A wise teacher saw the struggle and said: "I remember when I first made a sock puppet I could never figure out *how* to put on the eyes with only one hand. Now let me see . . . what did I do? Oh, I think I know . . . " The teacher went on to fill a detergent bottle with sand and began talking her way through each step. She pulled the sock over the bottle (all the equipment was on the table) and fastened the button eyes on with bread bag twist sealers. The child watched intently and then proceeded to experiment with a whole new set of options. The tone was one of: here's an idea that might help—there's no right or wrong, just a different way to go about a task, and you can try it or invent your own way.

Time

Time is also an important element of tone setting. Children become more deeply engaged and invested in their projects if they have the time to explore something of interest in considerable depth. Too often a child's school day is so full of transitions and interruptions that sustained time for one project is rare. This is a tremendous detriment to developing a child's concentration and learning. Research has shown that since the arrival of television, children's attention spans are about as long as a segment between commercials! Our school schedules only exacerbate the situation.

Time is also an element in the duration of accessibility to many materials. Some programs whip out a new material each day: clay one day, wood scraps one day, and sewing one day. They are then boxed up and put away for another time later in the month. Having the same materials out over an extended period invites children to master, invent, and expand on their ideas. When certain materials are available for long periods, children turn to them as needed resources for their projects. Sometimes just seeing the material will spark an idea for the needed airplane wing, puppet nose, or magic wand. It takes a keen awareness of what materials are being used and how they are being used to know when to introduce new sources and combinations and when to put away others for awhile.

Attitude and Atmosphere

An attitude and atmosphere of acceptance are essential for children to feel comfortable in their attempts to try new ways, to take risks, share their ideas, and develop flexible thinking. For example: The teacher is making plaster and gauze masks with the class. They are messy masks and need to cover the child's face while being formed. A few children want a mask, but are not at all comfortable with the medium or with having their face involved in the process. If the atmosphere in the room is one of acceptance, then the teacher can make available alternative routes for making a mask: paper bags, paper plates, boxes, or other wonderful options yet to be invented by the children. As adults, we need to keep the spontaneous expression of children unencumbered by our preconceived notion that, for example, what a child draws in the left side of Figure 6–3 should, in reality, be what is shown on the right side. Children will only explore the materials in any room and use them creatively if an attitude of respect and acceptance supports the child's experimentation. Parents sometimes need help understanding children's attempts to represent their world. They need to be reassured that what children do is a process and that this process and willingness to try are what counts. A workshop or exhibit showing stages of their art development as well as other available resources help parents to appreciate and understand all that is involved in a child's work.

Diversity

We need to ensure that materials reflect the diversity of families in our schools and in our lives. Every child needs to feel welcomed, comfortable, and accepted in the classroom. It is important to encourage children to bring things from their homes or for teachers to supply things that are familiar to them (labels in all languages and written symbols; pictures, magazines, and books of many cultures; empty food boxes for the dramatic play area that include different ethnic cuisines; dress-up clothes that represent what their families really wear). It is equally important for all children to experience these differences and become comfortable and aware of their own feelings. Making crutches, walkers, leg braces, and hearing aids available in the room gives children a chance to discover and better understand what it is like to need such equipment to function in the world. Though these materials open up the possibilities for many avenues of exploration, the underlying attitude in the room is what creates the deeper substance.

Presentation

A certain spirit of delivery and investment of energy by adults conveys a subtle but powerful influence on the climate of a setting. One home child-care provider, who has remained in touch with the simple joys that children experience when adults join in their world, exudes just such a spirit. Her whole house is a stage and unbelievable things turn into costumes. The most unique feature, though, is her fairy glue pot. This caregiver is undaunted by the meager funds available for materials. She found, as we all do, that for young children, the joy in gluing is more in watching the dripping process than it is in adhering two substances. Glue, unfortunately, is also expensive. This clever lady invented the individual fairy glue pot. It's a tiny container made from a strip of paper bag about three-fourths of an inch wide and three to four inches long. It is wound around a finger into a cylinder then glued to a

Figure 6–3
The spontaneous expression of a child must be
unencumbered by the adult's preconceived notion
that the child's attempt to draw a human figure
(i.e. the one on the left) should look like the drawing on the right.

small base of cardboard. It holds just enough glue to do whatever project the children are working on (refills are possible, of course) and the magic of it is they never feel deprived for having such a small portion. Instead they delight in the presentation and the charm of using a fairy's glue pot.

Material Gathering: A Smorgasbord for Idea Making

Most schools have a limited budget for materials, which encourages an interesting mix of the commercial and homemade variety. It is this author's belief that both are necessary, but I'd prefer to discuss the use of recycled materials as I believe their value is often underestimated. They can be an excellent resource for both the adults and the children in the room. If the adult uses them to create learning devices, it's important to make them aesthetically pleasing and safe. An example might be the use of colorful plastic bottle tops for game markers versus the metal screw-off tops that are ugly and have sharp edges. One also needs to look at the expense involved in making something aesthetically acceptable versus a commercial purchase. Covering a cardboard box with $15 worth of contact paper to create a play stove or sink might be penny-wise, but pound-foolish. Perhaps investing in a commercial set in the beginning would be more appropriate and save money in the long run. This is especially true if it is a popular item that will get much use.

Gathering collectible cast-offs or trash-to-treasure items requires the help of parents and children in saving and transporting such treasures for the class. Communicating and demonstrating the importance of these items to the children's development and the curriculum helps families begin to balance this with the constant media hype about high-priced toys "guaranteed" to better educate children. By modeling the intrinsic value of everyday, open-ended materials as viable learning tools in school, we are also encouraging a valuable link and continuity with their use at home.

The availability, storage, selection, and choice of materials is a critical consideration in managing any environment for young children. Children need to be able to see what is available, where it is stored, and what expectations are for the care, use, and clean up of such materials. Collections of tubes, bottle caps, yarn, jar lids, small

By modeling the intrinsic value of everyday open-ended materials as viable learning tools in school, we are encouraging a valuable link and continuity with their use at home. Here, toddlers ride the train, saying "I think I can!"

Modeling the use of graduated sizes of boxes, blocks, or other objects makes spontaneous storytelling a fun option for everyone.

boxes, cloth scraps, and the like can be stored in a variety of ways to be organized and accessible to the children and to make logical sense at clean-up time. These materials are a highly valued source of creative extensions to stories. Three different size boxes can represent the billy goats gruff, three bears, three pigs, and other trios. Dressing them, putting details on such as ears, wild hair, and so on are completely up to the children and often inspired by the availability of the materials, glue, tape, staples, hole punches, and other such supplies for attaching and transforming.

The following is a list of trash-to-treasure items to collect, display, and store for children to transform and combine in their marvelously unique ways. Guided by what they learn from past experience children build their own repertoire of ideas and thus demonstrate the world of possibilities. Suggested collections include:

Cast-offs:

- boxes (jewelry, Kleenex, cereal, shoe, toothpaste, oatmeal, etc.)
- film canisters
- jar lids
- paper tubes
- egg cartons
- foam rubber packaging
- sponges
- buttons
- baby food jars
- shower curtains
- socks
- scrap paper
- purses/wallets
- big boots
- dresses
- shirts
- detergent bottles
- see-through containers
- spools
- wood scraps
- cotton balls
- yarn
- popsicle sticks
- tongue depressors
- toothpicks

- old sheets
- Ping Pong balls
- tennis balls
- material scraps
- old jewelry (especially beads)
- hats
- nightgowns
- slips
- ties
- shoes

- toothpicks
- sandpaper scraps
- styrofoam chips and forms
- margarine cups
- serving trays
- magazines
- tents
- baskets
- shirt cardboard
- pipe cleaners

Nature's collectibles:

pine cones	shells	twigs
pods	rocks	pebbles
beans	seeds	straw
feathers	dried flowers	leaves
bark	horse chestnuts	acorns

Other Collectibles

Sometimes older siblings, friends, relatives, janitors, and senior citizens have collections they no longer want. Solicit for such things as: gumball machine trinkets, jack-in-the-box prizes, cards, miniature cars, dolls, dinosaurs, or the like. Take-aparts—old vacuums, windshield wiper motors, clocks, radios, typewriters, and fans—are wonderful sources of reusable materials.

Children have transformed these cast-offs and collectibles into body parts for robots, musical instruments, beds for the three bears and Corduroy, bridges, pretend food, puppets, billy goats, facial features, dollhouse furniture, miniature worlds, and so much more. Children have the ability to endow their playthings with significant meaning and to use them in magical ways to tell a story. Watching both their physical and cognitive skills evolve through the use of these open-ended materials justifies the collection and storage of all that "stuff." These recycled materials are truly more treasure than trash (see Figure 6–4).

Story Storage

Flannel Character Holders.   Staple up each side of a file folder, label, and carefully tuck characters in the "pocket." (This works best for adults; children tend to stuff it.) For children, it's best to store them in the flat lidded boxes that overhead projector sheets come in, or stationary and/or small pizza boxes.

Miniature World Storage.   Shoe boxes work well with a label or symbol of the story on top and on the exposed side of the box. Taking a photo of the pieces that go in the box and adhering it to the inside lid helps children check to see if they have all the pieces gathered for the next person who will use them.

Creating Story Props

Providing props for the various stories is a shared endeavor. The more variety, the more options everyone has to tell and retell a given story. A significant part of the

Figure 6–4
Trash-to-treasure storage containers

Shoe boxes:

Clearly label boxes and place them out on low shelves so the contents are easily seen and readily available. Putting the lids on the bottom reinforces the box and makes the lid readily available when you want to put it away.

Plastic detergent, milk, and cider jugs/containers:

Cut off tops of containers and thoroughly wash out the contents. Label with permanent markers. See-through plastic milk and cider jugs work particularly well. Another possibility is to cut a large opening on one side of the jug. The handle can then stay intact and allows the children to remove it from the shelf.

Many supermarkets now store their bulk candy in marvelous see-through plastic bins with removable "trap" doors in the front. They throw them out—but will save them for you if you make arrangements ahead of time. They stack and are fun to use!

Copy paper boxes:

Paper from commercial copying machines often comes packed in strong cardboard boxes with lids. Check local schools, churches, colleges, and business operations. Wood scraps, fabric, wallpaper, and the like can be neatly stored and labeled in these boxes.

Figure 6–4 (continued)

Wooden boxes:

You can obtain these free if you know someone at a liquor or import store that uses such boxes. Even if you need to buy them, the fee is small considering their durability and possible uses. I've found it hard to find shop owners who will "share" them, but I keep trying. They make excellent shelves or larger boxes for storing bulkier collections.

Large paper bags:

Two large paper bags (one inside the other) with their tops folded down create a quadruple-thickness storage space. These can be labeled colorfully and easily replaced when they wear out.

Deep box lids:

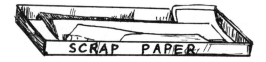

The best box lids to use for this are those from copy machine paper boxes. They are rectangular and allow spreading of materials for easy visibility.

Discarded drawers:

Sometimes drawers outlive old desks, dressers or kitchen cabinets. Save them—they make excellent, sturdy storage bins.

Figure 6–4 (continued)

Tool boxes, plastic ice trays, and egg cartons:

The components in these items make excellent storage units for buttons, beads, washers, and the like. Garage and farm sales often have old tool boxes. Wash out, dry thoroughly, and spray paint.

Gallon milk cartons:

Cut milk cartons in half lengthwise for small-item storage (clean them well!).

Other helpful small-item storage containers:

- small boxes that once held jewelry
- yogurt containers
- margarine tubs
- large cardboard ice cream containers from school cafeterias, ice cream stores, hospitals, and other places serving large quantities of food
- strawberry baskets.

journey is to live with a story for a week or two exploring it as a theme in variation. To do this, we tell the story using many different props. One day it might be a big book, flannel board, or puppets. On another day it could be boxes that become the three bears, or paper tubes, or the children themselves. The following section applies to teacher-created props for use by the adults and the children in the class. It's a good idea to construct two sets of flannel board characters, miniature world props, and anything you wish to keep in good order. We used to make up only one set, and it would become so dog-eared or incomplete that retelling was a frustration. All of this will take time. Encourage parents, friends, senior citizens, and any other talented individuals to help you create the variety. Children will use the trash-to-treasure items to create their own props if this is encouraged and respected as a valuable use of their time.

Books as Props

Japanese Story Cards

In Japan they are called "kameshibas," and they are a marvelous idea. The story illustrations are on the front of the card and the words are written on the back. This arrangement allows the reader to face the children and look right at them more easily than when holding a book off to one side. You can also hold up and rotate the cards around the circle so the children can see the pictures as you continue to read. To make a set of cards you need:

- plastic insert pages
- three rings
- oak tag cut slightly smaller than insert pages
- illustrations, magazine pictures, coloring book pictures, or the like

Cut the oak tag, and arrange story characters or scenes for each "page" of the story on each card with accompanying words on the back. When the glue is dry, slip oak tag into the plastic insert pages, order them in sequence, and attach with rings.

When a book has gone out of print, we check it out of the library, copy the whole thing (enlarging the pictures), color in the illustrations and make it into a story card set.

Big Books

When books become dog-eared or the bindings are no longer holding the pages together, pull the book apart and make a big book out of it. Cut off the frayed edges of the pictures and glue them onto oak tag. Write the story in larger print under the pictures to help those children interested in seeing the words as you read to them. Cover the pages with clear contact paper and use rings to bind the pages. The real advantage of a big book is the feeling of being "surrounded" by these large pages and having giant words to explore. For other book-making ideas, see Figure 6–5.

Puppets as Props

Anything can become a puppet if children have been encouraged to create and use their ingenuity. Having organized and treasured trash around will inspire creative features, limbs, and outfits. The suggestions in Figure 6–6 can be used as a base for children's unique ideas or for spontaneous storytelling when you'd like a quick prop.

Other Ideas for Story Props

Pegboard Easel Story Board

The pegboard easel story board (Figure 6–7) is a very versatile piece of equipment for storytelling, for use as a small manipulative board, and as a paint easel. Pegboard comes in many different lengths and with a variety of hole sizes. (If you want to use one side as a pegboard with golf tees, be sure to bring a golf tee to the hardware store with you so that you can get the right size hole.) Depending on space, storage, and number of children who will use it at one time, your size can vary greatly. I've used two pieces of pegboard measuring 22 by 24 inches with a different size hole on each side. Connect the boards together at the top with two shoelaces, leather strips, string, or the like. Ring binders also work very well. Tie the sides together at one edge to keep the boards from collapsing.

Figure 6–5
Other book-making ideas

Use the *cardboard backing* from writing tablets and cover them with cloth, colored paper, wallpaper, wrapping paper, or plain white paper. These will form the back and front covers of a book. Place paper in between the covers and hold together with staples, rings, shoelaces, or yarn.

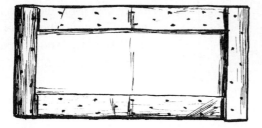

Fold a *clothing box* flat (as the retailers do to store their boxes). Glue a piece of paper over the folded sides. Take about 10 sheets of paper and lay them down on top of the paper you've just glued. Sew right down the middle of the paper. Fold in half and you have an instant book with box lid cover. Decorate cover with any of the ideas from above.

One teacher uses *old catalogues* for her class books. The children glue white paper over each page and the book is ready for use. It's sturdy, compact, and doesn't put all that colored ink into our environment!

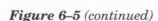
Figure 6–5 (continued)

Enclosing photos, old book pages, and the child's original work in ziplock plastic bags makes a useful book configuration. Place each page in a bag, zip it closed, and place one or two rings close to the "zipper" to hold the book together. Large snap clips also work to keep the book together.

Pegboard Flannel Board

Cut one piece of flannel about an inch larger all the way around than one panel of the pegboard. Hem the flannel. Cut four pieces of elastic and sew them to the back of each corner. These will then slip over each corner of the pegboard to form the removable flannel story board. Placing two of these easel story boards on the floor provides a divider in a room: story boards on one side and manipulatives on the other. You can also place them in the hallway for an announcement board or on a table for a different perspective.

Pegboard Paint Easel

Cover the board with plastic or aluminum foil for easy clean up. Attach paper with two clothespins and spread newspaper or an old shower curtain underneath for protection. Use a sponge with holes cut in it to hold film canisters with paint and a margarine tub with water. Set on a tray or box lid with brushes and a rag. This is an excellent surface for "painting a story" as you go along. Leo Lionni's *Little Blue and Little Yellow* lend themselves well to this type of easel.

Pegboard Manipulative Board

Select your hole size according to what you want children to be able to manipulate through the holes. The possibilities are endless. You might provide the following objects:

golf tees

telephone wire (this is particularly fun to add with beads, buttons, spools, anything with a hole)

shoelaces

yarn (with or without needles. Dipping one end of yarn or string into colorless nail polish will stiffen it to act very much like the end of a shoelace)

plastic-bag twists

Figure 6–6
Basic puppet ideas

Bag puppet: Lunch-size paper bags fit easily over a young child's hand and work well for a short-lived puppet.

Sock puppet: A child's sock is often more comfortable for the child to manage. However, it's fun to have a variety of sizes, since some love the big floppy look of an adult-size sock. Telephone wire cut in small pieces works well for attaching things to serve as eyes and nose.

Stick puppet: A child's drawing, tracing, or magazine pictures can be glued or stapled to a stick to create a very simple puppet. An upturned egg carton can hold the characters in place until "their part" comes in the reenactment.

Dangling puppet: Instead of gluing the character to the stick, punch a hole in the top of the character and reinforce with notebook reinforcers or tape. Then thread yarn, string, or elastic through the hole, knot one end and tie the other end to the stick. Now the puppet moves as the child wiggles the cord.

Figure 6–6 (continued)

Detergent bottle puppet: Any clean plastic bottle that will fit over a child's hand when the bottle's bottom is removed is fine for this puppet. If any of the edges are rough, just put masking or freezer tape around the newly cut edges. Have children really look at the shape of the bottles. Can they imagine animals, special people, robots, machines?

Cloth and ring puppets: This is one of the simplest ideas and requires only a small sheet or handkerchief scrap and a plastic curtain ring. It is particularly good for young children because the plastic ring helps to keep the puppet secure on the child's finger. The sheet scrap (about four by four inches) is placed over any finger and then the ring slips over the material and the finger. The child can add features to the puppet or can play with it as is.

Cup puppet: A styrofoam or paper cup is just the right size for a chid's hand to fit inside. The cup is the basis to which you can add other items for features and limbs. The cup can either be the whole puppet or just the head. A cloth scrap on the hand with the cup on top creates a head and body effect.

Figure 6–6 (continued)

Tube puppet: A toilet paper tube cut to all lengths can fit over a child's fingers and form an instant base for a puppet. It can also be used as antlers, legs, arms, or skinny bodies.

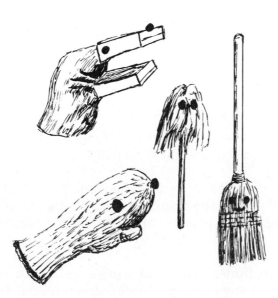

Mitt puppet: This is a more durable puppet made from an old scrap of sheeting, pillow case, or muslin. A paper pattern is made by tracing around a child's hand to form a "thumbless" mitten shape. Transfer this to material, then cut and sew around three sides. If a child is intrigued with a pattern idea, the concept of ears, hands, paws, and different-shaped bodies could be explored.

Other puppet base possibilities:
- rag dish mop
- dressed up broom (use handle to move puppet around)
- cereal boxes slipped over a hand
- sponge mitt (used to wash cars)
- mittens (the thumb can be the animal's ear or mouth)
- two gelatin boxes and a sock

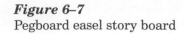

Figure 6–7
Pegboard easel story board

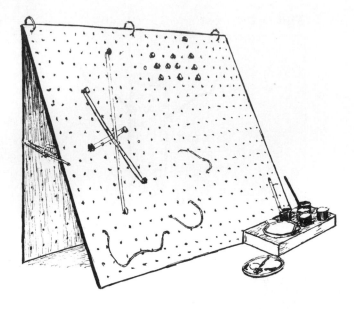

One child cleverly filled the pegboard with golf tees, pulled out certain ones randomly down the face of the board and rolled table tennis balls and larger marbles through the open spaces. It was a hit with everyone and opened up a whole new realm of ideas.

Another child took the class button collection over to the easel and with telephone wire retold the story of *Frog and Toad* and the lost button. He took a long piece of wire and as he told the story he poked the wire through a different hole making a big loop to hold all the various buttons that frog found for toad—one with two holes, another with four holes, thick ones, thin ones, different colors, and so on. As he spun the story it was as if the wire was traveling on a path through the woods. One *never* knows what will evolve as an inspiring story "place."

Felt/Flannel Story Board

The flannel board offers a simple medium for children to retell a story either alone or with others. There are a variety of ways this can be made:

Cigar Box Stories.   The lid of a cigar box provides a good place to glue a piece of flannel or felt. Felt is more expensive, but it does not fray and tends to hold a little more securely. The box itself can hold the characters for the story replay. This is also a good container for travel. A book and flannel pieces of the story characters make this a fun birthday or going-away present for a child.

Masonite.   Cut two pieces of masonite 12 by 9 inches, and fasten the pieces with two small two-inch hinges. Measure the flannel one inch larger all around the opened board so that it can be folded over on all sides and be secured with wide postage tape.

Velcro Board.   A special, substantial material works well with velcro and is another source for a variation in story replay. I order this material from Creative Educational Surplus. This supplier also has rolls of velcro with an adhesive on one side so that you can attach anything to it for storytelling. Cut the material to the same measurement as one pegboard panel. Attach four elastic strips to the back just as you did with the flannel *or* attach with four small squares of the velcro, which you can stick on all four corners of the pegboard.

Magnetic Boards. Anything that holds a magnet can become a story board: the refrigerator, file cabinet, radiator cover, hospital bed bars. Portable versions can be cookie tins, the old large reel film canisters, baking sheets, stove mats, metal shelves, and so on. The stove mat is the safest and lightest for young children. It measures about 14 by 18 inches and costs approximately four dollars in most stores. It leans up against the pegboard easel and provides another way to vary the retelling of a story. To secure the stove mat to the pegboard, you can temporarily attach small strips of velcro on the back to match up with the velcro tabs on the pegboard.

One magnetic tape has adhesive on the back that can attach to any character you may want to use on the metal surface. This tape is available in fabric, hardware, and novelty stores. (It is also available at Creative Educational Surplus, which is a discount supplier.)

One family found that their child was very content to play on the floor using the refrigerator as her story board. She would tell stories while mom and dad prepared dinner. When they went on a vacation they took a series of pictures, starting with packing, loading the car, eating at a restaurant, arriving at Grandma's apartment, going to the zoo in Grandma's town, and so forth. They did the "double special" when they were developed and covered one set with contact paper and put magnetic tape on the back of each photo. Now Lauren could relive her trip in story form and place the photos in sequence across the refrigerator door. It's a marvelous learning tool strengthened by the young child's concrete experience, egocentrism, and interest.

Story Characters or Props to Use on Boards

Felt pieces and pellon material will adhere to a flannel or felt board on their own. Just cut out the shapes, characters, or props you desire. With pellon you can use magic markers for the details.

Other Suggestions for Story Character Props

- photographs
- magazine pictures
- coloring books
- the children's own drawings
- two copies of the same book (old ones from garage sales, store closings, etc.)
- commercial flannel sets of stories

Cover each paper or tagboard character with clear contact paper for longevity. Attach any of the following to the back of each piece so they will stay up on the story board:

- strips of coarse sandpaper
- small piece of Velcro
- small wad of tic tac (used to hold pictures up without marring walls)

Make Your Own Slides for Storytelling

This experience is for children who are ready to become involved in a process that requires a series of steps and the ability to draw in a small space without feeling frustrated. (We did this with a group of five- and six-year-olds, and they loved it.) We practiced on pieces of paper that had boxes the same size as the slide dimensions, an inch by an inch and a half. It was a challenge to keep inside the squares when the children were used to drawing on *whole* pieces of paper. Some really liked drawing tiny figures in one square, others drew "designs," and a few ventured to put together a series of illustrated slides to go with their story. As each child would finish a slide or slide series, they'd come over to the projector and see them "come alive" on the wall while they'd tell their story to anyone who would listen.

   You'll need:

- transparent slide paper (overhead projector sheets work)
- slide encasements
- special pens (overhead projector pen)

These are best purchased at a photo supply store, unless you are familiar with the process and can order materials from a catalog.

Flashlight and Cellophane Windows

For telling stories where color is an integral part of the story line, it's interesting to tell it with paints, markers, colored paper, or with cellophane "windows." The lightweight cellophane can be wrapped around a cardboard tube (toilet paper, paper towel, or larger commercial cardboard spools) and secured with tape or rubber bands. Another idea is to cut holes in pieces of strong cardboard (approximately three inches in circumference) and tape heavy-duty cellophane (like the gels they use in stage lighting or the colored plastic theme paper folders) over the holes. (The gels cast a much stronger color.) A flashlight inserted into the tubes or placed behind the colored cellophane gels will cast that color on the white walls or ceiling. In retelling the stories of *The Great Blueness* or *Little Blue and Little Yellow*, this is a particularly meaningful extension. For *Little Blue and Little Yellow*, we tape two pieces of cardboard together to form a "hinge" with yellow cellophane on one side and blue on the other. When Yellow and Blue hug each other, we then close the two pieces of cardboard together and the spot on the wall turns green. This process has a certain magic quality that intrigues the children and they are interested in later experimentation on their own.

Miniature Worlds

Miniature worlds are just what the words convey. They are small versions of the story props that children can use to retell the story alone, in small groups, or with the whole group. Children can create their own or use those created or gathered by the adults. It's wonderful to see how children assign new meaning to the materials available. Children are often drawn to opposites—either very little or very big versions of characters. With storage a chronic problem, we've naturally concentrated more on the miniatures, but there is great value in giant characters, too. One day we told the story of *Rumpelstiltskin* with action figures fashioned from puzzle piece figures and dressed-up *Star Wars* characters. Princess Leia made a wonderful miller's daughter and the children tolerated the transformation. The castle was built of blocks and the spinning wheel for the miniature figures was actually a disguised, broken, toy motorcycle, turned upside down and lodged between two blocks. The children were drawn to retelling this story by the appeal of the miniature world and the characters of *Rumpelstiltskin*.

Other Miniature World Ideas

Graduated boxes, rocks, detergent bottles, wood scraps, jar lids, and the like can become the Three Bears, the Three Billy Goats, or any characters that come in varying sizes. If children watch you model this spontaneous use of materials, they'll be inclined to do the same thing.

Small Bottles

Hotels often provide shampoo, conditioner, body lotion types, and other toiletries in small bottles with round tops. These make fine bases for small characters. Adding felt features can enhance their realness and usher children into the replay.

Cardboard Figures

Cardboard story figures are a very simple, inexpensive way to develop miniature worlds. Start by cutting a one and a half-inch-wide strip of cardboard to a length of about 24 inches. Then form it into a triangle with a double strip on the bottom. The double strip is stapled together on the bottom to make it stand up more easily. Copy the desired illustrations from the storybook and mount them on the triangle base. They can stand unassisted, but are easily moved around as the story is being told.

Cardboard Box

A large cardboard box, stuffed animals, and small furniture create another type of manipulative for reenactment. One teacher set up a large box and cut one side down to form a platform. The teacher then cut out a small window in the back and glued black paper with holes punched in it over the window. The light came through the holes and looked like stars. A bunny was placed in a small rocker, a picture of a cow jumping over the moon was hung up on "the wall," and the scene was set for telling *Good Night Moon*.

Puzzle Pieces and Other Miniatures

There is no end to the possibilities and not all of them need be homemade. Puzzle pieces of figures, miniatures from family collections, garage sale items, and commercial sets are all available. One catalog that has particularly charming trolls, billy goats, other characters, and doll furniture is *Hearthsong* (address listed in under resources in Chapter 10).

Doing "giant" worlds is also a fun variation. Big figures of anything are fascinating for young children. Borrowing the clothes of the biggest dad in the room, stuffing them with newspaper, and fashioning a head out of a pillow case was one group's project for creating a life-size puppet of the giant in *Jack and the Beanstalk*. For one child in the room it was very comforting because he felt a sense of control over *this* giant. He didn't talk unless Johnny made him talk and he didn't stomp through the room unless Johnny got someone to help him move the giant. Another class tied a rope to two belt loops on the pants, one on the back of the giant's collar, and one to each knee. They dangled him from the second floor landing and in no time mastered the art of making him walk. It was fascinating to watch the group process and cooperation. Learning does occur in some of the most spontaneous, enjoyable ways!

Child's Own Gestures as Props

An interesting thought is the use of a child's own gestures, posture, expressions, and large body movements as a prop. Peggy Hackney (1988) states: " . . . the first step in any creative process is the art of merging, identifying, and becoming one with that which is there to be known. Young children learn through identifying. They learn the nature of 'cat' through becoming one." Reenacting trolls, giants, mean witches, and fairy godmothers requires that a child begin to identify with that character and try to move and act in such a way that it communicates how each of these characters might feel. It deepens the child's understanding by doing and physically makes internal thoughts and feelings external. It reveals the child's observational skills, attention to detail, experiences, and ability to integrate and act upon a wealth of information. Don't you think children would enjoy being a "living prop" and seeing themselves as a miniature world that's come to life?

Constructive Responding

Feedback can come from the children themselves, their peers, or the adults in their lives. How young children respond to each other and are responded to by the adults that are significant to them can have a powerful effect. It is an arduous task to balance one's response in such a way that it encourages children and stretches them in real ways without slipping into global praise or crushing the sensitive ego. Accepting their spontaneous attempts and upping the ante are a real challenge.

David Hawkins (1970) talks about the creative capacity for synthesis, for building a framework for assembling coherent episodes of experience. Prop building provides the chance to do this in many different modalities and to practice, invent, internalize, and master the process and the story. This chapter has suggested many ways to provide the capacity for this synthesis, but I believe it was important to briefly share some thoughts on the feedback loop in this process. If we organize these thoughts in terms of the "I" words (interaction, intervention, integration, and interference), it might help us to keep them in mind as we work with children and also *our* peers! The following discussion of these aspects of feedback explains guidelines that are comfortable for me. You may want to discuss or change them to work for you.

Interaction

Communication occurs to the extent that others understand one's thoughts, actions, and feelings. Sometimes it does not involve spoken language. As adults, then, it's important in our interactions with children to be sensitive to what they are doing, to observe and to quietly understand what is going on before moving into their world or agenda. We are joining children on their terms.

Intervention

An interaction becomes an intervention when another idea is interjected to extend on the child's thoughts, actions, or prop-building process. It's a supportive nudge to open up other possibilities. Sometimes children become stuck and need opportunities to see other alternatives or choices. It might be different ways to build things, rearrange their form, change the ending to stories, or interact with others. The ability for adults to know *when* and *how* to intervene is the essence of sensitive teaching.

Integration

Children gather information from many different sources. Our observation of their prop and material transformations as well as their interactions/dramatizations with peers and adults will give us many clues as to how they are integrating the story information.

Interference

We all know what happens here. The adult/child agenda becomes blurred and we intrude in ways that are not in the child's best interest. Our intentions are usually noble, but we lose track of who is creating.

John Holt expressed a similar philosophy when he stated:

> The adult's role is to provide the environment, to see that materials are accessible, and then to give children the opportunity to explore and think for themselves. In this process, the adult must learn *when* and *how* to intervene, for the intervention is crucial to the dialogue. In this process it is not so much the adult's knowledge of scientific principles that enables him to play his role skillfully, but his ability to establish the climate which everyone . . . adults and children . . . are encouraged to engage in the quest of wondering, relating, experimenting, discovering, and thus learning.

We all learn in our endeavors with small children. Their novel approach to life and materials can often rekindle our distracted curiosity.

*T*hose of us who pre-
sume to teach must not
assume that we know how
each child begins to learn.

~Vivian Gussin Paley

Traveling with the Team
Collaborating to Map Out the Journey

This chapter will

- *build an understanding of the role and significance of a team approach to planning and implementing all aspects of a journey.*
- *explore both the importance of team input and the mechanics of planning a story-book journey.*
- *develop guideposts and implementation for the planning procedure.*
- *demonstrate a variety of brainstorming process sheets and weekly plan sheets.*
- *link the planning procedures to the developmental implications.*

BEGINNING THOUGHTS

Developing a program that gives children both the security of a plan and the freedom to make constructive choices is essential! When children feel in control of their lives, it greatly enhances their energy for learning and potential for developing human relationships. The task of planning for such a program then becomes one in which children's learning is at the very core. This is in contrast to planning the "things" that children must learn. In other words, one philosophy looks to the curriculum for the core of its planning, while the other looks to the children. One measures success through prescribed formats and statistics; the other through human contact, personal pursuit, and an individual's growth over time.

An old version of *Webster's New Collegiate Dictionary* defined the word curriculum as "[L, a running racecourse, fr. currere to run.] a course of study. . . ." Based on my observations in many different schools over the years, a racecourse image for most curricula seems appropriate. The pace and frenzy that one often feels as educators and parents push for academics earlier and earlier in young children's lives has all the pressure of a race and leaves many youngsters in a cloud of dust along the sidelines. On a racecourse one must follow the pack, go in one direction, and be judged against "the best" or the *first* one to reach the finish line. For many, to reach the "finish line" is to have had the experience, but missed the meaning. The question to explore is who decides in education, anyway, what the finish line means and where the finish line is to be placed? Ann Wiseman (1973) put it very well:

> If you think that we are each original combinations of genes that have never existed before you must pause with wonder as a new child strives to become himself. But in our haste to get things done, be efficient, save time, keep the schedule and avoid harm, we rush children through childhood. For we are a very busy culture with little time for quiet thought or contemplation. It takes immense patience to allow children to learn at their own pace and through their own mistakes. Perhaps it is only vanity for us to think we can better past cultures by jumping to maturity without having exercised growth. (p. 10)

How often we rush children through the paces. So intent are we in covering certain materials that we leave little time for children to assimilate the meaning or to demonstrate their unique approach and understanding. Many curriculums have breadth, but little depth. We've all seen the caterpillar model on some classroom walls in which each segment of the caterpillar's body holds the title of a book that the class has read. The emphasis seems to be on numbers read; not enjoyment or understanding or a desire to read it three times because there was so much to learn, relish, or wonder about.

There is an interesting fable that illustrates what happens when a curriculum is so intent on *teaching* the material to be covered that it disregards the originality of each of its "children." This curriculum fable that I want to share with you seems less a fable upon each reading. It illustrates a curriculum that requires the same level of participation in the same course of study regardless of the individuals' talents, interests, or special challenges.

A Curriculum Fable
Author Unknown

One time the animals had a school. The curriculum consisted of running, climbing, flying, and swimming, and all the animals took all the subjects.

The Duck was good in swimming, better in fact than his instructor, and he made passing grades in flying, but he was practically hopeless in running. Because he was low in this subject he was made to stay in after school and drop his swimming class in order to practice running. He kept this up until he was only average in swimming. But average is acceptable, so nobody worried except the Duck.

The Eagle was considered a problem pupil and was disciplined severely. He beat all the others to the top of the tree in climbing class, but he used his own way of getting there.

The Rabbit started out at the top of the class in running, but he had a nervous breakdown and had to drop out of school on account of so much make-up work in swimming.

The Squirrel led the climbing class, but his flying teacher made him start his flying lesson from the ground up instead of the top of the tree down, and he developed charley horses from over-exertion at the take-off and began getting C's in climbing and D's in running.

The practiced Prairie Dogs apprenticed their offspring to a Badger when the school authorities refused to add digging to the curriculum.

At the end of the year, an abnormal eel, that could swim fairly well, run, climb, and fly a little, was made valedictorian.

Too many children are going to a school where the curriculum reads much like this dramatic fable! A colleague was exploring the word *curriculum* in a number of different sources and learned that the Latin derivative meant "to journey." That wonderful discovery opened up a whole new path for this project, for the journey meant finding pathways and avenues to learning, individual routes to mastery, passages into places unknown! It also meant we could all venture into the same territory via different roads and discover its wonders with our own style of gathering and using the information. As more of our schools begin to move toward including all children in regular classrooms, planning for the diverse strategies of learning and children's individual needs will become even more critical to the success of each child. The role of adults in education will change. Parents, support staff, and teachers will be much more involved in teaming up, consulting, and seeking each others' advice and expertise.

Storybook journey planning provides a framework for drawing on the talents of all those who work with children in a particular group or classroom. It is a planning process that invites everyone's input, interests, and expertise. The success of constructing and implementing such a planning process depends on our ability:

1. To invest our energy more in the learning process than in the teaching.
2. To learn about each child in the context of the family as well as in the context of the classroom.
3. To look honestly at what we value and begin to understand how that is actualized in the classroom.
4. To be aware of the full developmental spectrum of our children and to match their individual needs and interests with the plans.
5. To trust children's ability to select their mode of learning with support, guidance, facilitation, and modeling from adults.
6. To advocate and implement peer modeling and cooperative learning.
7. To encourage the meaningful interactions of the team. The team includes all the people in the children's lives: families, teachers, support staff, directors, principals, peers, volunteers, and others.

8. To create a rich environment with appropriate choices and varied options for learning.

THE IMPORTANCE OF PLANNING: MAPPING THE JOURNEY

In the storybook journey, the program plans serve as a guide sheet or reference map for weekly travels with stories as a group and as individuals. They record the generated ideas for inviting children to engage in activities of their own choice. They also encourage incorporating the story into every aspect of the day. Some of the activities help children internalize the story through many different modalities. Other activities are extensions of the children's individual pursuits and/or variations on materials that are always available to them: blocks, sensory materials, art tools, dramatic play props, manipulatives, and the like.

As part of planning, it's important to gather everyone who has any interaction with the children in the classroom or a vested interest in developing ideas on a particular story or subject. Input from these individuals enriches the planning dynamics and development. If you have any support staff members (occupational therapist, speech pathologist, psychologist, supervisors, parent, etc.) whom you can consult during the planning process, you can stretch everyone's thinking to focus in on all aspects of a child's development. This type of collaborative planning also serves to give each team member a real sense of what is being developed in the room and a certain ownership in setting up the environment and becoming more intimately involved in all aspects of the program.

An important aspect of the written plan is that it provides a means for us to track where we are headed and whether we are getting there as anticipated or have ventured off on other routes. The plan documents the organization of ideas around a story and individualized suggestions for the children before the journey. Briefly summarizing the events of the completed week on the back of the plans or in some designated space gives the team a chance to review the week, expand certain activities, change others, and share observations on the children's involvement before going on to the next week. This is a very informal way to evaluate the process and to document highlights, pitfalls, or new approaches and extensions whenever the story is repeated.

Storybook Planning Procedure

The planning process is a dynamic part of this journey. It requires at least a weekly meeting to brainstorm and discuss ideas, gather materials, and incorporate the needs of specific children. Many programs struggle with finding a time when all staff members can get together. Various schedules, other commitments, coverage of rooms, and endless other circumstances can prevent the team from scheduling a planning session. Because this process is so vital, however, the team should make it a priority. Work toward setting aside a specific time each week when all persons involved in the children's school life can be on hand. Notice the statement was "work toward" a weekly planning session with the team. If that is impossible, start with once a month. Figure 7–14 offers one suggestion for groups with limited meeting time. It is very hard for the support staff to "own" what is going on in a classroom when these individuals have not been a part of the planning process. If you teach alone, gather with other teachers in your setting and brainstorm together. Though you may take the story in many different directions, this gives you a chance to share each other's experiences, expertise, environmental setups, and use of materials.

Implementation of the storybook journey plans will vary from setting to setting depending on the children and families served, the staff/team configuration, and the time the children will spend in that setting (all day, half day, all week, certain days, etc.). Each group will need to decide how much of the journey can realistically be incorporated into the ongoing program. The guide sheets in Figure 7–1 are a means of organizing ideas that have worked for many centers and schools. Use them as basic forms to help direct your understanding of the process in the event you want to journey with your team.

DETAILS OF THE PLANNING PROCESS

Planning Sheet Examples

In moving from the brainstorming exercise to the weeks' plans, it is important to note that not everything generated in the brainstorming process can or should be used in one week. Many teachers go into more depth and extensions over a two-week period or as long as the children are involved or engaged in the story. There is no time limit! In most settings for young children a week offers sufficient exposure, but the choice is very individual. If you meet with children for only an hour and a half twice a week, you'll probably want to stay with a story for more than a week. If you're in child care all day, five days a week, however, daily involvement with the story is much greater. In the elementary grades some teachers have supported in-depth explorations of stories and gone off in all directions as the children's curiosity and interests have created many individual research projects. (One classroom did the story of *A Thousand Cranes* and developed a year-long relationship with a group of children in Japan, writing letters, sending folded paper cranes to each other to unite their efforts for peace, exchanging family photographs, etc.). There are no limits to the extensions, possibilities, or duration of time for one story.

DEVELOPMENTAL IMPLICATIONS: LINKING THE PLANNING PROCEDURE TO EARLY LEARNING AND HUMAN RELATIONSHIPS

The developmental implications of the storybook journey are a critical part of the planning procedure. They actually link the mechanical process of planning to the vital aspects of early learning and human relationships. The intention of this section is to define the implications as they relate to the use of stories and specifically to the journey process.

Rhythm of the Words

The earliest exposure to literacy is the parent or caregiver's voice uttering simple sounds, verses, or songs while rocking, changing, feeding, or bathing the child. It lulls children into listening, exploring, and playing with the sounds of their language. For example,

- The use of clapping, knee tapping, drum beats, or other instruments helps to accentuate the rhythm of the words and allows us to experience the pulse in two dimensions: with our ears and our bodies. (To many of us it's three-dimensional; rhythm touches our souls!)

• Combining large motor movement with words also enhances the rhythm and speech connection. For example, say the chant of the *Five Little Monkeys Jumping on the Bed* while jumping on a trampoline, cot, or pillows.

Repetition for Mastery

David Weikart (1979) states:

> One of the most important kinds of developmental progress that young children can make is their ability to represent their knowledge of the world in many different modalities and media. (p. 170)

Experiencing a story in many different forms with exposure over time becomes a scaffold on which children can build knowledge. Reading, telling, singing, acting out, and listening all add new dimensions to a child's enjoyment and comprehension of the story. Moreover, it isn't just repeated readings and telling of the story, but *how* it is read or told! For the experience to be meaningful and effective, it must be an interpersonal event of shared engagement, shaped by those who participate in it.

By providing various modalities, the child selects, models, or demonstrates the most comfortable means of internalizing and mastering the elements of a story. Some children must have a variety of materials to choose from for this mastery and retelling process.

Children—through their repetitive play with story themes—rehearse, practice, and master the joys and vital aspects of a story. Our response is important and can take the form of quiet, knowledgeable observation and attentive listening.

Repeated readings and "tellings" of favorite stories provide children with a treasury of words to hear and talk about, reinforcing and expanding the meaning, use, and enjoyment of those stories.

Predictability

Predictability follows so well on the heels of mastery because once a child masters a story, it becomes predictable. When children can anticipate and recall what comes next, it provides a safe way to participate: When the wolf knocks on the door, Little Red's grandmother is going to say: "Lift up the latch, my dear, and come in." They can anticipate what comes next.

Rebecca Edmiaston (1988) wrote that the characteristics of predictable stories include:

• Repetitive patterns
• Cumulative patterns
• Familiar concepts
• Good match between text and illustrations
• Familiarity of story or story line
• Familiar sequences
• Rhyme
• Language rhythms

Sequencing of Stories

To help children develop an appreciation and love of stories, it's important to start with the simple, repetitive ones and move on in complexity as the children are ready to do so. This progression has more to do with ability and temperament than with the child's age. Some very young children relish long, more complex stories, while others only attend for short periods. When the styles and abilities of a group of children differ tremendously, those seeking a challenge will often make the simple more complex in a variety of ways. One child will make up new verses to "Humpty Dumpty," while another child will want to see the Humpty verse in writing and is thrilled when the teacher writes out each sentence on long tagboard strips so that he can line them up in order with her help.

Sequencing also includes developing and mastering the concept of a story's beginning, middle, and end. It's helpful to talk a little about the story, the people who authored and illustrated the book, and any little interesting tidbit that will set the stage for the "beginning." The middle part of the story is not always as easy to insert, but it is worth a try: For example, "This is the middle part of the story where the wolf pretends to be grandma. . . ." The third part of the sequence is often relished with an exclamation of: "THE END!" when the book is closed or the words appear on the last page.

Sequencing includes the ordering of a story line from memory, as well as the progression from simple to elaborated versions of retelling a given story. For example, one child may have the three bears simply "eating porridge," while another child may have the bears eating the "sticky, steaming, yucky porridge in wooden bowls."

Thematic Confidence

When children have had many chances to hear, "read," and play with a story, this experience enhances the progressive phases of their play. Puppets, flannel boards, miniature worlds, and other items provide the "rehearsal props" for children to use either on their own or with others with whom they are most comfortable. Evolving from solitary or parallel play with the story to reenactment with the group indicates a child's progressive confidence in moving from self to others in this thematic story replay. A spontaneous reenactment or a guided experience during group time can reveal what degree of confidence children have in reliving a story with their peers. A graduate student's journal shared just such an observation. This was written in regard to a troubled little girl's retelling of "Little Red Riding Hood" during group with her own original puppets: " . . . for Jackie it is often hard to speak up on her own—maybe too much of a risk—but in the group she may feel more comfortable in speaking up for the wolf when her voice is but one part of a chorus of voices." We are always aware of the more confident children and relish those captured moments when their less-confident colleagues find their own secure way to be a part of the story replay.

Practicing Narrative Discourse

Being able to play the characters in familiar stories allows for the art and practice of narrative discourse. Children exchange a succession of happenings they have grown to know through various experiences with a storybook plot. The stories actually become a scaffold or framework for supporting children's attempts to relate to each other around a known theme and to practice communicating by acting out what they know and remember, or by improvising.

Basic Vocabulary Building

Sometimes we forget just how basic a young child's word knowledge may be. If we go merrily along reading stories without pausing to see if a child questions what they've heard, we may be missing an important step. A child interrupted the reading of *Corduroy Bear* one day to ask: "What is a night watchman?" The teacher asked: "Would anyone like to answer Matthew's question?" Another child proudly announced: "A night watchman watches the night to make sure that the moon comes up and that the stars come out to shine!" It provided a lovely discussion topic and a meaningful exploration of a word the teacher assumed they knew and was so grateful that Matthew had questioned.

As in every aspect of learning, if we can relate vocabulary to the young child's experience, its meaning becomes relevant and its use natural.

Expanding World Knowledge Through Schema and Scripts

The more information and experiences children have, the stronger will be their foundation for constructing a comprehension of the world. The story is most effective when accompanied by experience that will help the child develop schema—a mental sketch of how the world works; a way of organizing thought. "To know" the schema or script of a restaurant scenario, one needs the experience of "restaurant" (being seated, reading a menu, placing an order, etc.). Young children need the chance to role play the restaurant experience. Then, when they hear a story about someone eating out, they can further organize their concepts and thinking around such an event and build on their personal knowledge.

Nothing brought this home more clearly than the time a four-year-old child with a hearing impairment wrought havoc in the "department" store that had been set up for the play extension to *Corduroy Bear*. Jordan had shopped with his parents, but was always confined to his stroller. He had had the experience of going through the store, but missed the meaning of shopping. The script of looking, checking prices, selecting what you want, paying for it, and so on were not a part of his schema. In our play area, he would bag everything, dump it on the floor, rebag it, race around the room, dart back to the store, toss everything on the floor, and leave. He'd bypass the cashier, oblivious to the other children, their roles, maybe even their existence. It was such an eye opener for both his parents and the staff. As a result, his mother bravely let him out of the stroller on a number of planned trips to the store and conscientiously took him through all the steps to help him select and purchase a toy. In class he gave new attention to the wordless book, *Good Dog Carl Goes Shopping*, and his ability to "play" store took on significant meaning. Allowing him out of his stroller and taking him through the process helped organize his thoughts on how a store really works. This also altered the family's shopping trips significantly, since Jordan refused to get in the stroller again! Connecting stories with the child's experiences creates the conditions for children to internalize the meaning and to understand the language and life in context.

Providing the Stage for Creative Extensions

The plot of a story can create a safe platform from which children can launch or venture into making up their own versions or endings to existing tales. It might be as simple as changing *The Hungry Caterpillar* into a "Hungry Dinosaur" or as fascinating as one little boy's rendition of "Jack and the Beanstalk": "Well . . . the giant went down the beanstalk and asked Jack's mother to marry him and move to his castle . . . she has to bring all the things Jack stole from him!" When asked what would happen to the wife the giant is already married to, the little boy quickly answered: "Oh, she'll be the cook and live happily ever after. Oh, I forgot . . . we'll put her on a cot in the kitchen—no problem!"

Using an existing story line as the springboard, the child practices the story form in variations and gradually becomes more and more adventuresome. After awhile, only remnants of the original will show through, as children's own creations emerge. Observing this transition and supporting its development is an important part of literacy learning. From telling you their stories to writing them down on their own is a slowly evolving process that is a privilege to observe and facilitate.

Peer Interaction/Socialization

The storybook journey provides a connecting link for children of varying abilities in a number of ways:

Common Knowledge

As we are exploring a story together, we have that story line as our common thread. For children who cannot speak, but have seen and heard the story in a number of different modalities, that story becomes a bridge connecting them to their speaking peers. They can communicate that they want to be Red Riding Hood by dressing up in one of the capes and joining the other Little Reds for reenactment. (It's fun to have more than one person for each character in "the play!") By going along with a speaking peer, all children can share the enjoyment and feel safe to join in at their own comfort level. It provides a wonderful vehicle for socialization, acceptance, and meaningful interaction.

Perhaps it's important to note here that the spontaneous themes of play—rocket ships, house, bus, dinosaurs, and the like—often have many quick transformations or transitions in content that peers usually communicate with certain rapid-fire verbal cues. By this I mean that children usually offer quick, brief explanations of what is happening, often communicated while they are in motion (e.g., "Let's pretend the house is a spaceship now," and the next thing you know, the spaceship everyone was riding in is suddenly shifted to a bus). The average child can negotiate, accept, understand, or question these transitions. The child who has significant challenges with communication is lost. A story reenactment, on the other hand, becomes a valuable social tool for these children to take those first meaningful steps into play with their peers. The story provides the content that they can master and use to be a part of the social milieu.

Group Time

The story, in some form, is often the pivotal point of group time for those on a journey. It provides peer camaraderie, sharing of a common topic, and the focus for a discussion. Leading such a group time requires the teacher to span the developmental spectrum, reconceptualizing or signing the information as necessary so that all children feel they are an integral part of the experience. This is particularly challenging when the discussion focuses on the feelings of some of the characters in the stories. Talking about the characters' feelings lays the groundwork for comforting a child during times of difficulty. To be able to identify with Corduroy's feelings of being left behind by Lisa (when mom leaves you at preschool) or Humpty Dumpty (when you fall), or Eeyore (when everything is kind of in the dumps) is extremely helpful. It was heartening to see when, after one of those "feelings" discussions at group, a child fell off the swing on the playground and another child rushed to his rescue, put his arms around him, and said: "You fell off the wall, Humpty—are you okay?" It's the belief of this author that spending time with stories, retelling them in many different ways, and discussing the characters' feelings in a group provides a conduit for children to connect with each other in meaningful ways.

Environmental Components

The environment is an integral part of the journey. It supports every aspect of the child's development: encouraging physical challenges through play, psychological comfort and safety, cognitive pursuits, invitations to communicate, and support in learning to be a social being. The environment should offer a learning/relating/feeling space in which children strive to become all they can with the support of caring adults, both at school and at home. Realistic story props such as beds, blankets, bowls, and bridges can help organize the perceptual space and allow development of an area as grandma's home or the giant's castle. Children who are ready to move on to imagined or symbolic props can freely go about their reenactments in other parts of the room. It helps all children to have options available for their own adaptations and a certain ownership of the room to free them to create their own story settings.

Family and Community Partnerships/Links to Home

It has been well documented that when parents model naturally occurring literacy events at home on a daily basis, their children have a special advantage when they start school. Children seeing their family engaged in reading, writing, and communicating will attribute importance to these activities and be more likely to want to emulate this behavior. As teachers, it's important to communicate the significance of these events at home and also what is happening in school. The parent/school connection is vital to foster extended understanding of the developing literacy process and the role that home and school play in supporting the child's learning.

Links to Home Can Be Through

1. A weekly newsletter that includes a copy of the story each week; activities scheduled to support that particular story; needed props, and the availability of extra books, tapes, or miniature worlds that families can borrow.
2. Workshops to share the wealth of experience that can be developed and provided at home and at school to enhance the children's language and literacy learning.
3. Open pathways for families and community to be part of your program such as:

A parent's participation in the classroom helps create a strong link between home and school. This mother helped children build twig frames and stretch their muslin "canvas" for painting.

a. inviting parents to come read to the children; tell stories from their child-hoods; share their professions, hobbies, and interests; and demonstrate reading and writing as it relates to directions, recipes for cooking, sewing, putting machines together, and the like.

b. welcoming siblings to come and read with the children, especially when they have a day off from school.

c. inviting families (especially siblings) to send in tapes or books that they have enjoyed for sharing with the whole class.

d. encouraging community people to read to the children: Imagine the modeling and feelings involved in having the police officer, fire fighter, doctor, mechanic, mail carrier coming to *read* to you. It might be interesting to have them show the children how reading and writing affect their jobs (e.g., forms, reports, instructions, and the like).

Taking into account the interests and needs of the children and interweaving the themes of each story into the curriculum shows that the whole experience can go far beyond the literacy aspects of a story! The story's significant role, if thoughtfully mapped out by the team, is played out in all the developmental aspects of growing up: the social learnings, the physical feats, the awareness and sharing of feelings, the ability to reenact and communicate around a common plot, and the grappling with the many problems that surface during story replay. The plans the team creates are the road maps that incorporate all the above and create alternative routes essential for including all learning styles and abilities. These plans take time, energy, and a very real commitment to learning—our learning, the children's learning, and the learning of the team!

The following forms and charts will help you plan your lessons weekly and monthly:

1. Blank brainstorming sheets
   - Storybook Journey #I (Figure 7–2)
   - Storybook Journey #II (Figure 7–3)
   - Storybook Journey—Toddlers (Figure 7–4)
2. Making story connections: an explanation of the brainstorming sheet (Figure 7–5)
3. Sample brainstorming sheet: "The Three Billy Goats Gruff" (Figure 7–6)
4. Ongoing program essentials for young children: a checklist (Figure 7–7)
5. Blank plan sheet examples/options:
   - Toddler Planning Sheet (Figure 7–8)
   - Child Language Center Plan Sheet (three days a week) (Figure 7–9)
   - Storybook Adaptation Sheet (Figure 7–10)
   - Storybook Journey (four days a week) (Figure 7–11)
   - Northglenn Plan Sheet (Figure 7–13)
6. Sample plan sheet: "The Three Billy Goats Gruff" (Figure 7–12)
7. Storybook Journey Monthly Plan Sheet (Figure 7–14)
8. The storybook of the week alert sample: One way to welcome input from team members—including families (Figure 7–15)

Figure 7–1
Considerations in the planning procedure

Guideposts	Implementation
1. *Organize:* Effective planning takes commitment and time! Organize the schedule to devote at least one hour a week to creating the framework for the week ahead.	The storybook journey planning process has a progression of steps. They are laid out in this fashion only to help clarify the process, not to lock you into a formula. They are as follows:

I. **Find the story you want to use with the children.** Chapter 9 contains list of stories that many groups have enjoyed. The book list ranges from the simplest to the more complex. Refer to children, families, and colleagues for other suggestions.

II. **Read the story together and listen for concepts, themes, and ideas that can be encouraged during a journey.**

III. **Use the Story Related Brainstorming Sheets (i.e., Figures 7–2, 7–3, and 7–4).** These sheets are used for an organized way to gather ideas. The sheets are numbered I and II and offer a choice. Figure 7–2 has labeled the centers used in most classrooms for young children. In Figure 7–3, most of the boxes have been left untitled for personal use by various programs or therapies. One speech pathologist used the empty boxes to highlight the particular speech and language opportunities that each story presented.

IV. **Check over the *ongoing program essentials* (Figure 7–7) for young children.** This sheet offers a quick check and explanation of all the other important activities that are available to the children whether they are linked to the story plans or not.

V. **Select the ideas that would work for your age group and time frame.** Transfer those ideas from the brainstorming sheet onto the plan sheet. Examples of plan forms are included for your perusal.

VI. **Delegate gathering of materials.** Each team member can help locate the various pieces of equipment or materials needed for the story expansions.

VII. **Discuss environmental changes, extensions, and additions.** The environmental setups enhance every aspect of the storybook journey. Staging the dramatic play area as a re-creation of the house of *The Three Bears* or bringing in rafts and fish nets for *Wynkin, Blynkin and Nod* helps create interest and engagement with all the children.

VIII. **Connect with the family.** For many families, bringing things from home to use for a story can mean concrete involvement. Newsletters, notes, phone calls, chatting before class, the Storybook Alert Form (Figure 7–15), or the like can be used to help this process. Many programs include the whole story with their weekly newsletter so that

Figure 7–1 (continued)

Guideposts	Implementation
	families have access to the version used in the classroom. (If a family is non-English speaking or illiterate, a tape of the story in English or the family's first language is essential.)
	IX. **Try the Storybook of the Week Alert Form (Figure 7–15) if you wish to foster input from the various team members (including families and volunteers) who cannot make it to the planning sessions.** This is a useful way to help involve people who share the lives of your classroom children.
	X. **Evaluate the activities of the past week.** Use the back of the plan sheets (Figures 7–2, 7–3, and 7–4) for evaluation. Jot notes on the overall week's activities to help plan connections to the week ahead or to remind the team of activities, ideas, or things to avoid during the next journey.
2. *Involve:* Encourage the participation and use the expertise of all people who are involved in the classroom. Bring in significant people if you are exploring new territory or a specific topic. Planning for the diversity in learning styles, pace, cultural/ethnic awareness building, experiences, and interests takes all the help you can gather. Ideas contributed from the following experts etc. have been invaluable: • parents • occupational therapists • speech-language therapists • psychologists • other teachers/colleagues/paraprofessionals • principals, directors, supervisors • children • certain occupations: doctors, beauticians, secretaries, janitors, mechanics, farmers, police officers, fire fighters, etc.	• Invite anyone working in the room or others who share time with any of your children to plan with you on a regular basis. • For those who cannot attend, elicit their input either through a note or by using the Storybook Alert Form (Figure 7–15). • Occupational therapists and speech-language therapists can offer excellent suggestions in terms of physical challenges in the room around the story themes or unique ways to extend or encourage language in replay. • Parents have a wealth of ideas and expertise to be tapped: cooking, computers, animals to share, story telling, puppetry, magic tricks, professions, and the like. Inviting them to plan with you is a very real connection. • Children are very capable of helping to plan and need to have their ideas valued! Brainstorming works best with small groups or with individual children who have a particular interest. They often have unique suggestions and offer props they have at home. (Dictating or writing a note home to their families to remember what they will bring is a meaningful literacy link.) • In one setting, a doctor came to visit and brought his four-year-old daughter with him so the children could see that doctors can also be daddies. He read the story of *Curious George Goes to the Hospital* and then let the children play with the special things he brought in his bag—stethoscope, blood pressure gauge, "knee tapper" for muscle reflex, and various types of bandages. The questions they asked were extensive!

Figure 7–1 *(continued)*

Guideposts	Implementation
3. *Observe:* Children are individuals who need to be observed to be understood. Study the interests, frustrations, learning styles, issues, and struggles of each child. Sharing these observations is a critical part of debriefing sessions and the planning process.	• Choose stories that will expand and extend their interests, generate new ideas, and support them through their struggles. • Rotate and display a variety of books throughout the room for children to look at or have read to them during the day. This invites the children to relive their favorites or discover new ones they may not have been exposed to in the past. Stories can offer the children a level of comfort in knowing that others have struggles and interests similar to their own.
4. *Discuss:* Schedule time when individual children can be discussed in a "debriefing" session to assess their needs, interests, personal issues, and ways to extend their learning. The journey is only successful if each child finds a pathway that makes sense to him/her! Document these discussions in a notebook, journal, or on tape for a record of the child's growth over time.	• At the end of the week, it is strongly suggested that the classroom staff gather for approximately 20 to 30 minutes to discuss individual children. If this is not possible, try to record notes from your observations and interactions. • I believe that no adult should teach a group of young children alone! No human being can tune into all the needs and personalities that are evident in a classroom—especially a classroom that includes *all* children. The debriefing at the end of the week or writing in notebook by everyone who participated is far more valid when a number of people have observed the same child. • If we are to develop engaged learners and thinkers, we need a team of invested adults to facilitate and interact with children to encompass their diverse interests and individual needs. Discussion among the team members is essential to the process. If you are teaching alone, perhaps a parent volunteer, a college student volunteer, a senior citizen, or a peer teacher might share with you once a week for a designated time.
5. *Create:* Generate fresh ideas rather than pull out last year's plans around a particular story.	• Use the brainstorming sheet to build a whole new repertoire of ideas for implementation of the story extensions. It is a mechanism for gathering ideas, resources, and connections. (Since many of the classics are repeated year after year, it would be easy to pull out the old plans and say, "done!" This stale approach is *absolutely* discouraged!) • Old plans are checked out and reviewed only at the end of the planning session just in case something was not tried the year before, or if a successful idea could be expanded on in a new way.

Figure 7-1 *(continued)*

Guideposts	Implementation
6. *Reflect:* Explore your own memories about some of the things you enjoyed that might spark a new interest or extend the meaning of a story.	• Tell stories to the children from your past experiences that relate to the story. (One teacher who grew up on a farm shared a story and photographs of herself and her sister dressing up three baby pigs and using their dog to be the wolf. The children were entranced!) • As a child, I *loved* playing with anything that was a miniature version of the real world. I had a tiny metal replica of a wood-burning stove with tiny pans, kettles, and skillets; it even had a handle that slipped into a hole in one of the stove plates so that you could "stoke the fire." This love inspired creating miniature worlds for each of the stories as one more option for replay in the journey.
7. *Enjoy!* It is so much more fun to brainstorm and plan around a story with other people. We've had some good laughs and gone off on many tangents with this process. It certainly beats the "ho hum—What can we do this week?" syndrome! Energy and a fresh approach become contagious.	• The brainstorming process helps to "gather the harvest" and reap the benefits of others' experiences and expertise. • Share ideas, be open to exploring new territory, stimulate each other's thinking, and encourage everyone's participation. • Charlotte Winsor said: "Play is the process by which the child's experience is expressed and organized." In short, "planning" is the process of organizing and expressing the adults' experience and knowledge to offer invitations of choice to the children.

Figure 7-2
Story-related brainstorming sheet: Storybook Journey I

Cooking/Snacks

Sensory

Feel • Hear • Smell • Taste • See

Outdoor Play/Motor

Group/Individual Story Experiences

Miniature worlds, puppets, stand ups, action figures, song, movement, discussions, sharing, demonstration

Dramatic play/prop building/ Environmental set-ups

Extensions beyond classrooms

Related books, poems, stories

Literacy links

Construction

Manipulatives, blocks, Legos, puzzles, etc.

Art Experiences from Story

Family Connections

Science/Math

Understanding Diversity

THEMES/CONCEPTS:

STORY:

Figure 7–3
Story-related brainstorming sheet: Storybook Journey II

Group/Individual Story Experiences

Miniature worlds, puppets, stand ups, action figure, song, movement, discussions, sharing, demonstration

Dramatic play/prop building/ Environmental set-ups

Extensions beyond classrooms

Related books, poems, stories

Literacy links

THEMES/CONCEPTS:

STORY:

Figure 7–4
Toddler brainstorming sheet

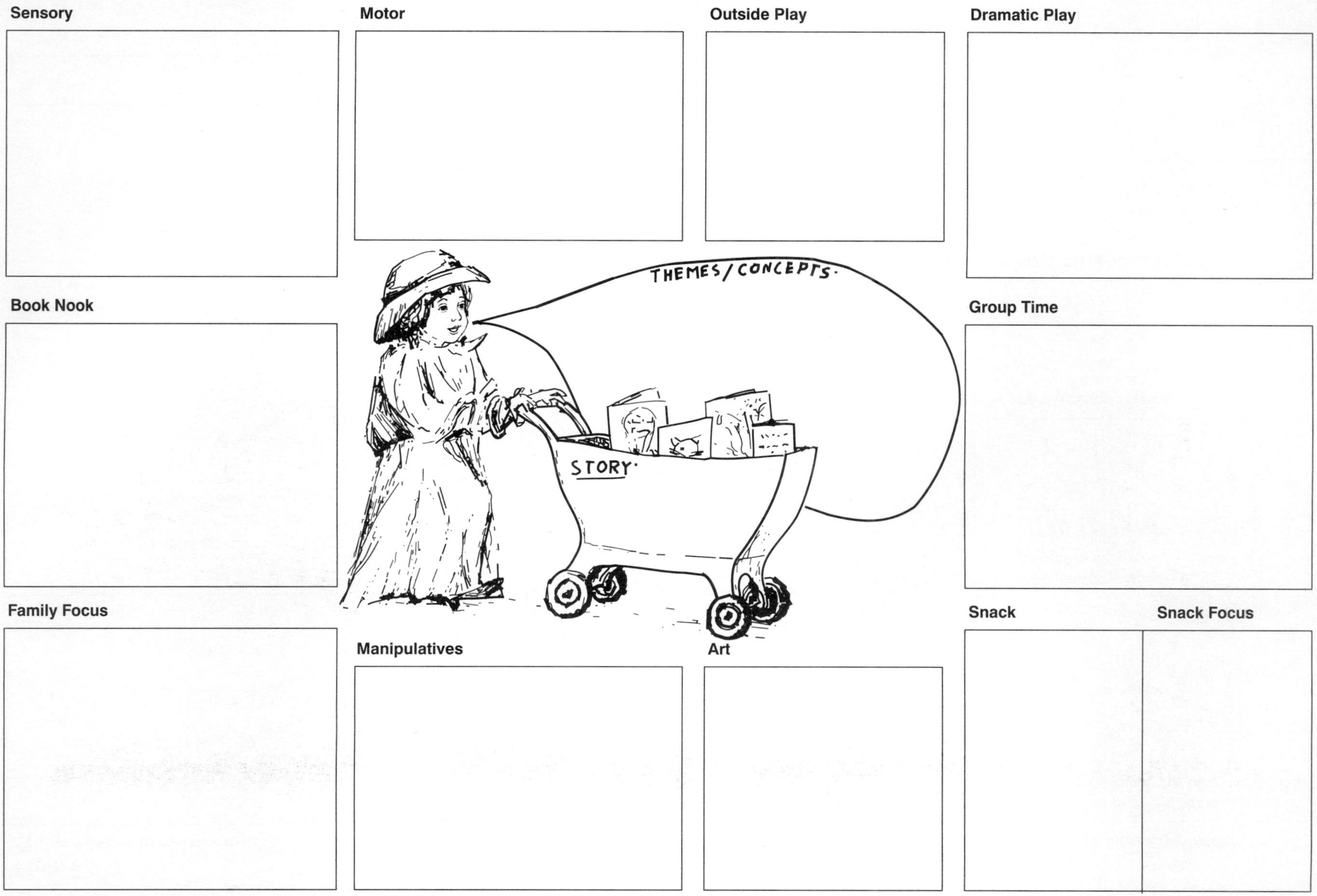

Sensory

Motor

Book Nook

Outside Play

THEMES/CONCEPTS

STORY

Family Focus

Manipulatives

Art

Dramatic Play

Group Time

Snack

Snack Focus

Art on a muslin sheet sewn to stick frames.

Snack time *for these toddlers includes trying chamomile tea with big cups just like Peter Rabbit.*

Construction *of houses for "The Three Little Pigs" replay.*

Sensory *delight in a lowered sand table.*

Figure 7–5
Making story connections through hands-on exploration: An explanation of the brainstorming sheet

Targeted Experiences	Making Story Connections Through Hands-on Exploration (an explanation of the brainstorming sheet)
Themes/concepts	The balloon portion of the brainstorming sheet is reserved for listing the concepts or themes elicited from the stories. (Story connection example: For *Red Riding Hood,* the list could include such things as red, head coverings, talking to strangers, aging, caring for someone who is ill, forests/woodlands, etc.)
Cooking/snacks	Cooking can be an engaging learning experience for children. The setup needs to be carefully planned to maximize the children's participation and learning. The idea is to relate the snack and cooking activity to the story whenever feasible. (Story connection example: *Humpty Dumpty* was an egg so anything related to eggs would be appropriate—boiled eggs, trying different kinds of eggs, making "egg boats," etc.)
Construction: manipulatives, blocks, Legos, puzzles, etc.	Using a variety of manipulatives provides children with alternative ways to see relationships, patterns, represent their world, and to learn about balance, symmetry, classification, and shapes through trial and error. (Story connection example: Children make Lincoln Log, block, or Lego houses for three pigs or use hollow blocks to build a home big enough for three bears to enter.)
Art experiences related to the story	Art in the storybook journey is separated from a project. Art is the child's original use of paints, clay, crayons, pencils, markers, and collage materials. Art in the storybook journey is a chance to explore a medium that has been set up to enhance understanding of the story. (Story connection example: Only blue and yellow paints or materials at table or easel for extending Lionni's *Little Yellow and Little Blue* or a suggestion to make mean, ugly trolls out of clay with special tools for the story of *The Three Billy Goats Gruff*.)
Family connections	Meaningfully involving families in their children's lives at school helps to establish a partnership in learning. Newsletters, meetings, slide or video sharing of the children's day in school, and a personal note or phone call all help to make a connection to the family. Keeping families involved with the storybook journey specifically can be done in a number of ways: A photocopy of the story can be attached to the newsletter; families can read or act out the story at home, props can be shared both ways; and any member of the family can come and read, sing, or tell a story, help with material gathering, or borrow the story suitcase (a small kit with a taped version of the story in the language spoken at home, a book, and a miniature world. This is particularly helpful if a family is not literate or needs to have the story translated into another language.)
Sensory	The information we receive about the world comes to us through our sensory systems: of touch, taste, smell, sight, and sound. Providing experiences that stimulate and satisfy the child's sensory needs are an important part of our daily setup. Water, sand, snow, bird seed, shaving cream, and the like are all rotated in turn through our standing water table or provided in large plastic bins set up on the floor. (Story connection example: *Are You My Mother?* provides an obvious chance to experience many kinds of bird seed in the water table to dump and fill, sort, bury, and hide objects, and watch them slide through tilted cardboard/plastic tubes as well as listen to the sounds they create.) When you're finished, throw it out to the birds.

Figure 7–5 *(continued)*

Targeted Experiences	Making Story Connections Through Hands-on Exploration (an explanation of the brainstorming sheet)
Outdoor play	The outside environment provides an excellent arena for story play or reen-actment. A certain spontaneity is unleashed when children play outside. Sandboxes, bushes, stones, twigs, snow, water, leaves, rocks, trees, gardens, hills, logs, and walls are all potential props. (Story connection examples: Sand becomes porridge for *The Three Bears*; trees are Red Riding Hood's forest; bushes are haystacks for hiding Boy Blue or a makeshift stick house for one of the Three Pigs.)
Science	Young children are naturally curious and eager to understand their world through self-exploration and discovery over time. The challenge is to set up appropriate areas inside and outside for hands-on experiences. They must hold meaning to the children and allow for extensions to their growing knowledge of plants, animals, and changes through such things as cooking, awareness of weather, moon cycles, seasons, death, and so on. (Story connection example: *The Little Red Hen* provides a simple story that progresses from the planting of grain to the production of bread making. The extensions to science are many with growing seeds and tending the plants, harvesting wheat, grinding the grain, changes that occur during the cooking process, watching the bread rise, smelling it cooking, and so on. All kinds of grain in its plant and refined form would be fascinating to explore.)
Math	Math offers a way to order experiences. As adults we need to provide many varied opportunities for children to grapple with experiences that help them do two things: begin to understand what the problem is and to decide on possible ways to approach the problem. (Story connection example: One summer a group grew "bean stalks" for *Jack and the Bean Stalk* and found all kinds of ways to measure them—hands, shoes, their own bodies, string, marks on a paper strip and dated once a week to show growth over time, a ruler, a yardstick, and the like.)
Understanding diversity	Highlighting diversity as a part of the planning sheet has helped us to consciously search through the story themes and concepts for valuable ways to include the broadest understanding of diversity. The primary aim is to sensitively incorporate diversity into the curriculum in a way that is meaningful to the children. (Story connection example: In *Swimmy*, a little fish that looks and thinks differently from the other fish develops a peaceful strategy to save himself and his friends from an intruder. Through acting this out the children can experience the feeling of working together to cleverly solve a problem.
Group and individual story experiences	The group time is the only time our children gather as a class. In theory, the expectation is one of enjoyment, learning, and sharing the common knowledge of the story being explored that week. In practice, the group times vary according to the interests and engagement of the children. The plan may indicate to read, tell, sing, or dramatize the story, but if the children have an exciting project, art, or their own stories to share, then that becomes the main focus. The stories for group time are developed to expose children to the various ways stories can be told: by reading, oral tradition; using flannel/magnetic board, puppets, painting/crayon/marker mural rollers; creating a miniature world; listening to music; through sign language, movement; and acting them

Figure 7–5 (continued)

Targeted Experiences	Making Story Connections Through Hands-on Exploration (an explanation of the brainstorming sheet)
Group and individual story experiences *(continued)*	out. After a story has been told, props are made a part of the room so individual children or small groups can reenact the stories on their own. This provides a means to master, practice, socialize, and extend around the framework of a loved story. (Story connection example: Perhaps the most meaningful example is the one in which Matthew developed his own props to retell *The Three Billy Goats Gruff*. He used wood scraps for the bridge and the troll and three jar lids for the billy goats. He used these props to tell the story at group time as well as to anyone willing to listen after group.)
Dramatic play/ Prop building/ Environmental setups	This section of the brainstorming sheet is meant to focus attention on what materials need to be gathered so the children and team can develop props and set up a section of the environment to encourage story replay. What is available, and what needs to be borrowed or made that will help to create the setup for inviting story-related play? For many children, the available props provide the means for them to play out their own interests with the overlay of the story. (Story connection examples: All kinds of tubes can be gathered for horns or tails for the three billy goats; old sheets can be used to tie-dye butterfly wings for *The Very Hungry Caterpillar*'s metamorphosis or to use as tents for *Just Me and My Dad* or capes for *Peter Pan*. Boxes can be the houses for the three pigs. Simple "furniture" can be used to represent a bed, table, chair, and so on, for Little Red Riding Hood's grandmother's apartment or house.
Extensions beyond the classroom	Where can the class go or who can come visit to help extend story concepts, knowledge, and enjoyment? (Story connection example: Visiting the planetarium as an expansion of reading *Moon Cake*; observing pasta being made in a pasta carry-out to go with the story *Strega Nona*, or inviting musicians to come with selected instruments for the replay of *Peter and the Wolf* or the *Bremen Town Musicians*.
Related books, poems, and stories	A wide variety of books is available for children to peruse. A special part of the reading nook might feature different versions of the same story (e.g., there are about 10 or 11 versions of *The Three Bears*, or you may want to just emphasize "bearness" and display books about real bears or story bears: Corduroy, Paddington, Pooh, etc.).
Literacy links to story	Reading, writing, listening, and communicating are all a part of literacy. Think about *how* literacy can be brought into the story replay; for instance, a miniature world setup available with an audiotape so a nonverbal child can "act" out the story with the miniatures while hearing the story on tape; children writing (dictating) their own stories in a journal or notebook; or developing cozy places in the room that will encourage children to look through and enjoy all kinds of books. (Story connections or "additions": Papa Bear reads a paper, Mama Bear writes a shopping list or reads a recipe for porridge, all the bowls are labeled (Mama Bear, Baby Bear, etc.); children can make signs and post them in the woods for *Little Red Riding Hood* such as: "This way to grandma's," "one way," "stop to pick the flowers," "knock before entering," etc. Grannie's house could also have the address written on the mailbox — (Grandma Hood, 1 Forest Lane. It's a way of nudging awareness of environmental print and emphasizing that letters, words, and numbers hold meaning.)

Science involves studying a fish that had died in the tank.

Understanding and celebrating *diversity* through meaningful human relationships.

Literacy links include signing for a child with a hearing impairment during group time.

Dramatic play with a doctor's office scene. A nurse looks up the patient's name in an appointment book.

Figure 7-6
Story-related brainstorming sheet: "The Three Billy Goats Gruff"

THEMES/CONCEPTS:
- control of bad guy
- big, bigger, biggest
- little, medium, big
- over, under, off
- three
- feelings: fear, anger
- grass to straw/hay

Cooking/Snacks
- animal crackers
- goat's milk/cheese
- coconut dyed with food coloring (green and yellow for "straw and grass")
- alfalfa sprouts (grass)
- trail mix to represent "goat food"
- use goat cookie cutter on bread, cover w/cream cheese, olive for eye
- make up something fun that trolls love to eat

Sensory
Feel • Hear • Smell • Taste • See
- flour, sand, or cornmeal in bins with miniature figurines
- plant grass seed in bins for miniature world set-up
- water table with plank across top for bridge
- bring in real goat to feel, smell, observe, and listen to

Construction
Manipulatives, blocks, Legos, puzzles, etc.
- suggest bridge building with blocks, Legos, bristle blocks, boxes
- make trolls with Legos, bristle blocks, or anything from art area
- set up goats, miniature trolls, and gnomes in block area along with cellophane grass, props for water, etc.
- build farm for goats or a house for the trolls

Art Experiences from Story
- use of water color palettes
- make a troll on large piece of paper with individuals adding various parts to the troll (either collage or paint)
- make large mural including trolls, billy goats, grass, water, bridges, etc.

Family Connections
- help locate hay bales
- need volunteers to act out Three Billys for a video rendition of the story

Outdoor Play/Motor
- hay bales outside
- wooden planks to use with hay bales for building bridges
- bring out big blocks
- hose in and sand box with planks over the "streams" we'll make

Group/Individual Story Experiences
Miniature worlds, puppets, stand ups, action figures, song, movement, discussions, sharing, demonstration
- use 3 sizes of blocks or detergent bottles for goats with troll to tell story
- what instruments might sound like troll, goats, bridge walk, water
- walk across balance beam as if it were a bridge—beat drum to set a pace

Dramatic play/prop building
Environmental set-ups
- make horns and beards
- create yarn wigs for troll
- set up a variety of bridges to cross and let "goats" decide which bridge will challenge them

Extensions beyond classroom
- visit to goat farm
- bringing in a real goat
- walk to the stream

Related books, poems, stories
- bring in books about *real* goats and their habits, care, and so on

Literacy links
- listen to story on tape with books
- dictate different endings or extensions to story
- write notes like *Caution: Troll ahead* or troll's house to be posted by bridges
- in one version the troll is reading under the bridge!

Understanding Diversity
- differences in sizes & girth
- all brothers in same family of goats, but individuals in temperament
- discuss why the troll may act so differently from other "people"

Science/Math
- make cottage cheese (observe changes)
- prepare environment for goat's visit: what will he eat, drink, etc.
- sprout grass seed
- filed trip to goat farm or a stream
- sorting in category of 3
- use 3-ness in all set ups
- feature little, medium, big

STORY: "The Three Billy Goats Gruff"

Figure 7–7
Ongoing program essentials for young children: A checklist

The purpose of this sheet is to provide a quick check and explanation of all the other important activities that are available to the children on a daily basis. These activities are set up as an ever-present choice for the children whether they are linked to the story plans or not.

Art Center

A separate setup for the children's independent use and exploration. The presentation and offerings vary according to children's interests.

- paints (tempera, water color, finger paint)
- variety of utensils to paint with (brushes: house painting, water color and tooth brushes), sticks, cotton swabs, and so on.
- trash-to-treasure items for collages, sculptures, free forms (beads, wood scraps, fabric, paper scraps, telephone wire, jar lids, small boxes, etc.)
- markers, colored pencils, regular pencils, ballpoint pens
- glue, staples, masking tape, adhesive tape
- scissors, protractors, rulers
- Playdoh, clay, and tools to use with both
- assorted paper, cardboard, wood scraps

Block Area

Blocks are a valuable tool for constructing representations of the world, studying relationships, patterns, designs, balance, and for experimenting, planning, and playing! They need as much space as possible, free from traffic pathways. Blocks are a marvelous means of joining individuals in a group project or social endeavor. Organize blocks for visual cues and organized, independent clean up.

- check unit blocks to see if you have at least one complete set
- blocks come in all forms: large hollow blocks, unit blocks, cardboard bricks, large and small Legos, waffle construction blocks, and more. The most important ones are made of unpainted, finished wood, but if you cannot afford them, find substitutes as children need to build!

Woodworking and Take-Apart

Create a place for construction with wood and real tools. This area must be safe and supervised. It may need to be a special feature area, closed on days when supervision is low, but try to find a space for it. Safety glasses are highly recommended.

- various sizes of soft wood scraps (pine, poplar)
- screwdrivers (regular and Phillips), pliers, hammers
- hand drill with varying bits
- screws, nails, tacks
- hinges, corners, washers, C-clamps
- wire, spools, wheels, machine parts
- dowels
- old vacuum, typewriters, record players, clocks, hair dryer, windshield wiper motors, and more (all with plugs removed) are great for children to take apart and to use for construction projects.

Animals, Plants and Other Living Things

Learning to care for something that cannot survive in captivity without our taking the responsibility to feed, water, change cage, and so on is essential. There is also the realistic value of coping with death and dying as a process of life when children see fish and plants die.

- rotating classroom pets is a valuable experience. Being exposed to a number of species as well as caring for particular needs can teach priceless lessons. Many pet shops are willing to help you with this experience (for a price) if they are assured of your care practices.
- Pets that seem to do well on a permanent basis are fish in aerated tanks, guinea pigs, newts, hermit crabs, and snails. Worm and ant "villages" also do well if carefully maintained.
- plants, bulbs, bean seeds, vegetable tops, cuttings, and pits are fun to experiment with and add great warmth to a room when healthy.

Figure 7–7 (continued)

Sensory

"Messing about" with a variety of sensory experiences is stimulating and meaningful to young children. It involves touching, hearing, seeing, smelling, and tasting. Setups and materials will dictate what to do. Many programs keep their water table or large bins in use with a rotating variety of goodies at all times. Some of the most popular items are:

- water, mud, sand, dirt, snow
- bird seed, rice, pebbles, egg shells
- cornstarch (dry and with water)
- shaving cream, soap flakes (with water)
- accessories such as scoops, spoons, cups, sifters, detergent bottles, funnels, strainers, colanders, tubes, syphons

Cooking

Preparing food with children can be a very satisfying experience. In today's hurried world of fast foods and faster paces of living, many children do not have a chance to prepare food with their families. Observing changes, textures, processes, smells, recipe reading, and tasting are all very valuable ways of gaining and mastering new information.

- shell peanuts and make peanut butter with a food grinder
- break eggs, explore shells, beat own egg with egg beater and scramble for snack
- wash, peel, and chop veggies for soups and salads
- cook a whole chicken, peel meat off the bones and make chicken tortillas. Clean bones and dry them on paper towels. Surprise children and bury them in the sandbox for a "dinosaur" dig.
- expose children to a variety of tools: peelers, scrapers, nutcrackers, blenders, toasters, food processors, grinders, strainers, foley food mills, graters, and more.

Dramatic Play

Children want to try on the world of others as a way of mastering meaning. Setting up an area of the room that encourages a variety of role-taking possibilities requires planning and careful attention to storage, display, and clean up. Props for the following on a rotating basis will invite interesting play:

- doctor, dentist, or veterinarian office— include waiting room, magazines, nurse's station, secretary, receptionist
- firehouse
- barber/hair dresser/beautician (*Dandelion*)
- supermarket (*Mexicale Soup*)
- toy shop (*Corduroy*)
- office
- home replications (*Three Bears, Three Pigs*)
- shoe store (*Cinderella*)
- restaurants (especially McDonald's!)
- police station
- post office (*Jolly Postman, Frog and Toad are Friends*)
- car, airplane, bus (*Wheels on the Bus*)
- spaceship (*Moon Cake*)

(I couldn't resist making story connections with some of these!)

Gross Motor

Young children are creatures of action. No matter how small your space, provide some way for children to move their bodies in a variety of unstructured events. Have some of the following available:

- slides
- sawhorses
- tree stumps
- planks
- ramps
- scooter boards
- wheel toys
- parachutes
- tunnels (create or buy)
- balls (large and small)
- things to crawl over, around, through
- barrels
- hoops
- large wooden blocks
- large boxes
- roller skates
- bikes/trikes
- scarves & music
- bridges

Figure 7–8
Toddler planning sheet

Date:

Story:

	Tuesday	Thursday
Setting the Stage (Provide choices to invite children to try a variety of activities.)		
Snack and Social Focus (Create a calm, accepting atmosphere that encourages children to reach out to each other. To encourage socialization, plan a unique "focus" at the table, such as, a gold fish and bowl as a centerpiece, a pretend spider hanging from the ceiling, or a bug in a jar, etc.		
Outside Set-up (Arrange a variety of equipment in interesting, *safe* ways for children to explore.)		
Group Experience (Expose children to be with others for a brief shared experience—story, songs, etc.)		

Figure 7–9
Storybook journey plan sheet (three days/week)

STORY:

WEEK OF:	MONDAY	WEDNESDAY	FRIDAY
CENTER ACTIVITY			
SNACK			
OUTSIDE ACTIVITY			
GROUP ACTIVITY			
UNDERSTANDING DIVERSITY			

Figure 7–10
Storybook journey plan sheet with adaptations (three days/week)

STORY:

WEEK OF:	MONDAY	WEDNESDAY	FRIDAY
CENTER ACTIVITY			
Adaptations			
SNACK			
Adaptations			
OUTSIDE/MOTOR ACTIVITY			
Adaptations			
GROUP ACTIVITY			
Adaptations			
UNDERSTANDING DIVERSITY			
Adaptations			

Figure 7–11
Storybook journey plan sheet (four-day week; four-year-olds)

	Monday	Tuesday	Wednesday	Thursday
Open Choice				
Literacy Links				
Snack				
Outside				
Group				
Special Features				
End of Week Evaluation Notes				

Figure 7-12

Storybook journey plan sheet (four-day week; four-year-olds)

Week: Oct. 20 to Oct. 23   Story: *Three Billy Goats Gruff*   Group: p.m. preschool

	Monday	Tuesday	Wednesday	Thursday
Open Choice	Bird seed in water table with rubber goats, tongue depressors, and cubes for building bridges Individual paints at large table Brown, green, yellow added to easel Start alfalfa sprouts (T) Set up table for orange peeling and cut-up bananas (T) Set up Legos, bristle blocks	Set out bins of flour in water table with sifters (T) Put jar lids in 3 sizes and Fresh Start bottles in 3 sizes in water table Scramble eggs, break shells carefully, save (T) Collage: big troll, big table (T) Eye droppers, food coloring, and coffee filters on big table Playdough with scissors	Make horns & beards for props (T) Plant grass seed in empty shells (T) Miniature world set up in block corner Set up bridge planks in open area Prepare a special area for Norman the goat's visit on Thursday. Think ahead as to what he will need to be comfortable.	Straw, grass, rocks, sticks, rubber goats in water table Finish collage if needed (T) Troll puppets on tongue depressors (jar lids for billys) (T) Play with Norman in his special place (T)
Literacy Links	• Story on tape with books (3 children can listen at one time) • Sign posts, paper and special markers available for sign making	• Troll shape books for own stories in writing nook (Suggest: if I were a troll, this is what I'd look like and this is what I'd do!)	• Miniature world set up in quiet space for small group retelling	
Snack	Bananas & oranges (sliced, serve with toothpick), water	Scrambled eggs, toast (troll/monster toast recipe on bulletin board), milk	Wednesdays are set aside for family share-a-snack day.	Trail mix with green coconut as "grass," cranberry juice
Outside	Bikes, scooterboards, and barrels	• Bring big blocks and planks out for bridge building • Hose in sandbox.	• Climbers set up with ladder/hood attachments • Building with hay bales	
Group	Read story Start troll for collage	Miniature world story using 3 varying blocks and troll, block bridge (leave out for children to explore for rest of week).	Flannel board with emphasis on goat and troll's feelings in this story.	Act out story with Norman in the part outside Come in to see parent's video of the story before going home
Special Features	• The visit of Norman the goat • Building outside with hay bales		• If weather permits, Wednesday's schedule will be scratched and we'll visit the goat farm.	
End-of-Week Evaluation Notes				

T on this sheet represents teacher supervision needed. This icon helps us to see if we've set up too many activities at one time that require adult help.

Figure 7–13
Northglenn plan sheet

Teacher: Story:

P = Physical   L = Language Learning   A = Affective or Emotional   Y = Social

Date	Monday	Wednesday	Friday
Notes			
Room #1 Blocks/Toys Climber Workbench Free Art Water Table Easels			
Room #2 Science Story Corner Puppets Puzzles Project			
Room #3 Housekeeping Dramatic Plan Manipulatives			
Outdoors/Large Motor Water/Sand/Dirt Parachutes Obstacles Hoops/Tunnels/Teeter Marching			
Large Group Music Storybook Journey Film Strip Drama			
Small Group Language Stories Games Fingerplays Concepts and Fun!			

Figure 7–14
Storybook journey monthly plan sheet

Dates	Story	Linking Book Resources, Themes/Ideas to Pursue	Long-Range Plans/Organization

Figure 7–15
Storybook of the week alert form

The Storybook of the Week
Alert Form

Please take a moment to look over the plans for next week's story and share any suggestions or insights you might have.

The story of the week _____ to _____ is:

_____

Plans are attached and your input will be appreciated.

This week we need:

Please return to _____ mailbox by _____ .

Thank You!

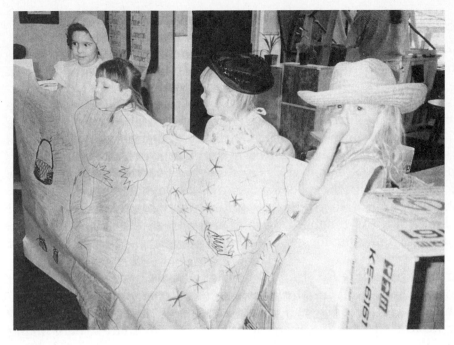

*L*iteracy is listening, learning, and quality of life. It is reading, writing, thinking, scribbling, drawing, and being motivated to find meaning. It is interpreting, inventing, associating, communicating, responding, sharing, and being able to set visions into action. Our challenge as educators is to make it possible for all children, regardless of ability, experience, or cultural heritage, to feel successful in their attempts to be literate.

~Sue McCord

Literacy Extensions

Interesting Expeditions in School and at Home

This chapter will be in three sections:

- *Literacy extensions of one story*
- *Literacy extensions grow from a wide variety of experiences, meaningful play, and through connections with families*
- *Story extensions as an approach to intervention and the inclusion of all children*

LITERACY EXTENSIONS OF ONE STORY

Varied experiences with telling a story and developing story extensions give children a sense of mastery without drill. These experiences create the capacity for a richer knowledge base and the satisfying personal engagement with hands-on participation. Each story contains any number of concepts that teachers can develop for young children. For example, the story of *Little Red Riding Hood* includes the concepts of red, talking to strangers, the woods, or bringing food to someone who is ill. Extensions are intended to involve children in play with all aspects of the curriculum, environment, choice of materials, and peer relationships. Extensions nudge children to experience and experiment in all the developmental domains: physical, cognitive, communicative, emotional, and social. Story extensions beyond the classroom to home and the community are a vital part of the total experience and a significant link bridging families, schools, care providers, and other support professionals.

Through a journey with *Little Red Riding Hood* we'll briefly explore immersion and the extension possibilities of this story with an emphasis on literacy. A workshop session with teachers, parents, and paraprofessionals generated many concepts and themes around "Little Red." The following section shares them, along with some ideas to think about for expanding a story in many meaningful directions.

Concepts/Themes in the Story of Little Red Riding Hood

Workshop participants are always amazed to see how many ideas begin to emerge once this process begins. Listing all the concepts and themes suggested by the story helps the group envision the possibilities for exploration in the curriculum.

Here is what evolved from one group that gathered to plan a journey with *Little Red Riding Hood*:

- red/colors
- forest
- strangers
- trust
- illness
- remedies for getting well
- caring
- baskets
- head coverings (hoods, nightcaps)
- wildlife
- doctor/veterinarian
- aging
- grandparents
- occupations
- wolves
- diversity (language, gradations of the color red, ages, what people like to eat when they're ill)

Literacy Expansion Ideas with Little Red Riding Hood

Taking the concepts and themes that have been generated, the gathered group then discusses how to weave these extensions into the curriculum, environment, materials, and parent participation. The following ideas are just suggestions of the possibilities *Little Red Riding Hood* presents.

Color

- Have children bring in something red. Set the items up in a special area for display and explore all the variations in color. Document the children's observations and comments.

- Put out red paint in six sections of an egg crate. In the other six sections line up white, blue, yellow, and so on. Encourage the children to experiment with what happens to red when you add other colors. Record their discoveries on videotapes, audiotapes, or in writing.

Letters and Language

- Have children dictate or write letters to their grandparents or an elderly neighbor. Maybe a letter could be attached encouraging the grandparents to write back about what they enjoy most about this time in their lives or what they are finding difficult about aging.
- Set up a mailbox outside of grandma's pretend house so the children can mail their "get-well" cards.
- Share all the children's different names for their grandparents: Nana, Gams, Grandmother, Grandma, Gramps, Grandfather, Grandpa, Pop-pop.
- Explore what various cultures call their grandparents.

Older Generation

Many children's books talk about our aging population. Here are a few excellent suggestions:

> *The Fall of Freddie the Leaf* (Leo Buscaglia)
> *Nana Upstairs & Nana Downstairs* (Tomie de Paola)
> *Now One Foot, Now the Other* (Tomie de Paola)
> *How Does It Feel to Be Old?* (Norma Farber)
> *Wilfrid Gordon McDonald Partridge* (Mem Fox)
> *The Midnight Eaters* (Amy Hest)
> *Grandpa, Me, and the Treehouse* (Barbara Kirk)
> *Annie and the Old One* (Miska Miles)
> *Happy Birthday Grampie* (Susan Pearson)
> *Sachiko Means Happiness* (Kimiko Sakai)
> *A Special Trade* (Sally Wittman)
> *I Know a Lady* (Charlotte Zolotow)

Have these books available for children to leaf through or have read to them. This is a very good preview, in a nonthreatening way, of some of the changes the children may experience with aging grandparents, great-grandparents, neighbors, and other aging friends in their lives.

Nursing Home Visit

Think through the process of doing a visit to a nursing home in the community with an eye and emphasis toward literacy. For example:

- Ask children how one might find a nursing home (i.e., yellow pages, ask mom, call hospital information).
- Ask how to find the closest one to the center or school (maps, ask around, relatives in a home).

- Once the nursing home has been found, there is planning: When do you go (check calendar for possible dates), what do you do when you're there (act out Little Red, sing), who do you contact to make arrangements (names, phone numbers)?
- Invite the residents to come to the "party" (given at the nursing home; where, when, time). Also invite parents to come along.
- Bake muffins for the nursing home with a simple recipe children can "read." Bring them in baskets.
- Have the local paper come so the children can "read" about themselves the next day.
- Act out the story for residents (sequencing and remembering what comes next).

All of these activities could stretch over weeks or just a few ideas could be incorporated depending on the group makeup, ages, and the classroom support.

Study Real Wolves

Decide what would be appropriate for your particular group. For example: There are videos, films, and books on wolves. Make a list of these resources. Locate a "local" wolf to observe in a zoo, pet store, or private residence. Find meaningful ways to share a better understanding of wolves, one that may overcome the poor image they have in literature. For fun, read books like *The True Story of the Three Little Pigs* by A. Wolf (as told by Jon Scieszka) or *The Wolf's Tale* by Della Rowland.

Veterinarians

Where does a wolf go if he is injured? Explore the role of veterinarians. Visit an office or have a vet come to school. Have vets tell the children what they had to learn to become a veterinarian. (You might combine this with a visit from wildlife preserve personnel.)

Baskets

Make a study of baskets. Look up the different kinds, where and how they are made, and what materials are used. Collect baskets and display them. This is a particularly meaningful way for cultural input, as many families may have baskets they have brought with them from their own countries or from their relatives or travels. Many may also know how to make baskets.

Head Coverings

Make a study of head coverings in our country (baseball caps, cowboy hats, visors, hard hats) and around the world. It is fascinating to know the history, customs, and reasons behind certain head coverings. A good book to start with in this exploration is *Hats, Hats, Hats* by Ann Morris.

Eyes and Ears and Teeth

The lines of: "what big eyes . . . what big ears . . . and what big teeth you have" create a perfect chance to have an optometrist/ophthalmologist, audiologist, or dentist come to school—or, better yet, to visit one of their offices. The importance of taking good care of one's eyes and ears can be stressed in relationship to learning. (Braille books and hearing aids would be natural to explore at this time, too.)

Feelings

Think about and discuss how each of the characters might feel and try acting out those feelings. Feelings give literacy its uniqueness. The children's drawings, paintings, writings, and interpretations have much to do with feelings. As an example, consider how the characters in *Little Red Riding Hood* might feel:

- Mom: Worried about sending Red Riding Hood through the woods alone? Worried about grandma's illness? Proud of Little Red's independence?
- Red Riding Hood: Afraid or happy to go by herself? Looking forward to time alone with grandma? Hoping she'll have some of the cookies Mom packed in the basket?
- Wolf: Playful? Mean? Angry? Hungry? Grumpy?
- Grandma: Anxious to see Little Red? Nervous? Frightened? Mad?
- Woodsman: Strong? Proud? Fearful? Brave?

You and the children will think of so many more extensions—and therein lies the treat. This example of ideas was only a nudge for your own brainstorming.

HOW LITERACY EXTENSIONS GROW

Dorothy Cohen (1972) said that children should be allowed to learn first from life, then from books. This section of the chapter will attempt to combine life experiences and books. It will playfully weave the essence of literacy into the play world of the child both at school and at home.

Everybody Reads

In learning to read, it is critically important for young children to interact with adults who are significant to them. Interactive storybook reading and storytelling between adults and children have powerful, lifelong results.

To encourage such interaction, suggest that the children's families turn off the television and set aside a 15- to 20-minute time each night when everyone reads a book, magazine, or newspaper alone. It can be a significant time for modeling the importance of "reading" and establish a habit for the later years when homework will demand the same attention.

Invite siblings, senior citizens, janitors, principals/directors, support staff, other teachers, secretaries, cooks, and others who are a part of the child's life to read different versions of the same story.

Individual reading times during the school day with a child are invaluable. This gives children a focused time to discuss their interests, questions, and extensions without interruptions. It is a very valuable time for building literacy foundations. Olympic wrestler Jeff Blotnick said that to read without discussion would be like "throwing the roses out the window without smelling them." Solo reading to children can be a wonderful gift from volunteers. It is an activity most of them feel very comfortable doing with the children.

Play extensions from a few stories that can incorporate "reading" and word awareness:

Waiting Room. Set up a physician's or dentist's waiting room with magazines and books, a desk with appointment book, phone, phone numbers, forms, bills (story connections: *Curious George Goes to the Hospital*, *Berenstein Bears Visit the Doctor*, Shel Silverstein's poem, "The Toothache").

Restaurants. Use of menus with pictures of food and words, restroom signs, order pads, bills.

Grocery Store.   Study labels, ads, directory, scales, cash register, price signs, grocery list (e.g., *Stone Soup, Mexicali Soup*).

Inside Bus, Subway.   Try reading advertisements, coin machines, newspapers, magazines, graffiti (then again, you might want to avoid reading that!). Many items outside the school bus offer chances for reading, too: stop flipper, school district name, emergency doors, license numbers, and so on (e.g., *Wheels on the Bus*).

Service Stations and Junkyards.   Check pumps, check oil, cash register, oil cans, signs, items in store or junkyard.

Everybody Writes

Create a print-rich environment and share an awareness with parents about all the writing possibilities that children can experience with their families. The more experiences children have with incidental environmental print, the more their play can meaningfully incorporate it. Suggest the various writing experiences that children can observe in the real world and play with in school and at home. Following are a few suggestions of things to place in the environment as "writing props" for play.

Write to Baby Doll.   One group of children had a baby and bear day. The children wrote stories for their baby dolls or favorite stuffed animals and "read" them to their companions when they brought them to school on this special day.

The teacher listens to what each child will bring for Stone Soup, draws a picture of that food, and writes the child's name beside it—a meaningful literacy link to the story.

The Mailbox.   In one classroom a mailbox was added to the cardboard house of "The Three Bears" to encourage writing letters to the bears.

Hints/Encouragements for Writing Throughout the Classroom.   Place notepaper and a pencil on the play refrigerator door; clipboards and pads in various places; pad and pencil by the phones; envelopes, stamps, and writing equipment near children's cubbies or mailboxes; a special writing carrel and/or office made from a cardboard box.

The Writing Carrel.   This carrel is made by cutting the top and bottom flaps off of a cardboard box. Cut one side from top to bottom. Open up. Cover with contact paper. Make holders for pencils, paper, rulers, crayons, markers, and so on out of the bottom part of detergent bottles. Fasten to box with brads. Constantly change or add to this carrel/office such things as: typewriter, adding machine, calculator, old checks, forms, receipts, protractors, staples, hole punch, brads, paper clips, telephone (with photo, name, and phone number for each child).

The Cloud.   Introduce children to the concept of the "cloud" to hold words that a person is saying or thinking. You can obtain stickers with these clouds in various sizes and shapes. The children are fascinated with the idea and anxious to "write" what their drawn characters have to say.

"Post-its."   These stick-on notes are also fascinating equipment for encouraging writing. Some children enjoy putting a word on them, sticking them to another piece of paper, and hiding a picture underneath the flap.

The Child's Journal.   In some settings, each child has a journal that is used and developed in various ways. Some classrooms have children write in it each day, others have special days. Some teachers leave the journal time completely child-directed, while others may ask for specific entries such as: draw/write about family news, describe something you saw on television, record the development over time of the bean growing project or the mice babies. One teacher put a colored cut-out blob on one page in the journal and had the children make up a story about this blob and illustrate it. The possibilities are endless.

Home/School Journal.   In one classroom, staff members keep a journal on each child that they transfer between school and home. The journal documents special events, issues, concerns, and celebrations both at home and at school. It represents a weekly exchange between the teacher and the family about the child. If time allows, it might be a nice review of a child's week if an adult in the room could include the child in making some of the entries. The children could be asked what they would like to tell their family about their week and the family could do the same in return, asking "What would you like the teacher to know about your week at home?"

Success Notebook.   One very sensitive little girl, whose ability to express herself was *very* limited, wanted so much to share the successes she'd had both in school and at home. Her parents devised the idea of sending a small notepad each day with a few sentences about B.'s evening successes: "B. set the table for family," "colored pictures while waiting for dinner," and so on. The teacher would read this aloud to B., make comments, and B. would beam. The teacher would then write a few sentences about B.'s day in school that the parents would read to B. at home. She began to develop much more positive behavior in school and at home with this focus on the positive *and* the shared communication between her two worlds.

Other Experiences.   Grocery lists, correspondence, invitations, notes and reminders to child or self, messages in lunch boxes, tickets, advertisements, garage sales, and car repair. Riding in the car is also a marvelous time to experience all the printed matter that surrounds the ride (stop signs, neon advertisements, license plates, billboards, street names, etc.).

Everybody Has a Story

Stories about one's own childhood or the childhoods of significant others are a very special part of feeling connected. They also represent a meaningful experience with literacy.

Family Stories.   It might be fun to tape record a story from each family about an interesting incident in the early life of their child. These stories could be typed into a book with photos or drawings. Children can then listen to the tape and look at the pictures together. (Of course, the story could be read to them, too.) This would be a meaningful connection to home.

Childhood Memories.   Childhood memories of parents, teachers, and other important adults in the children's lives would also be fun to record. Memories about pets, friends, siblings, houses, family, play times, or experiences growing up in foreign countries or on a farm, ranch, in the city, and the like would just be a few of the possibilities. (When I was teaching kindergarten, the children loved to hear about my childhood camping trip when a porcupine crawled up on my sleeping bag during the night and stayed their until I gave out a loud sneeze in the early morning.)

Home/School Connections

The home/school connection is often placed on the back burner as families and teachers become buried in their endless responsibilities. It is a fact of the times we live in and something we will just have to strive hard to schedule in as best we can. For young children, this relationship is very important: They need to see tangible evidence that home and school together have placed a value on learning. The following suggestions will take time, but are well worth the effort.

Transition Book.   Transitions are part of life, and children have their own unique ways of dealing with this process. Teachers and families can play a significant role in preparing children in advance and supporting them with concrete, meaningful information. Developing a book to introduce your classroom to incoming children is an effective transitional tool. The welcoming teacher can have a book ready for newcomers that will introduce the children to their future classroom. This book would be an excellent "transitional object" to leave behind on a home visit. The child could look it over later and ask her family questions, look for the familiar, and "visualize" herself in the new setting. Photographs are a good way to familiarize children with a new place. They are easily photocopied so that the cost of processing a book for all children would not be prohibitive. Ideas to share might be gathered from the outgoing class: "What do you think children coming here for the first time might like to know about this classroom?" Here are a few suggestions:

- pets that live in the class (gerbils, fish, pig)
- the bathroom
- private places for personals (cubbies, bins, or lockers)
- water table
- materials (books, markers, puzzles, Lego, blocks, dolls, cars, easels)
- equipment (minitrampoline, climber, big balls, bikes, computers)
- things to explore (beehives, ants, rocks)
- teachers, assistants, cooks, janitors, director/principal
- picture of school from the outside and the playground

Home Visit Book.   Take a picture of each child at the home visit to put in a book for school. For some children it might be a very helpful, immediate link from home visit to school. Pictures of themselves with other family members or with their pets are suggestions for eliciting beginning connections. A little write-up of the home visit for each child might help spark some memories; for example, "Remember when your dog barked so loudly when I rang the doorbell and wouldn't stop. . . mom had to put Scarfy in the basement."

Sally Rose Goes Home on the Weekends.   Sally Rose, named by a group of four-year-olds, is a stuffed white bear that travels to a different home each weekend with a class family. She goes home in a special bag with a journal. The idea is for Sally Rose's "hosts" to record the adventures of Sally Rose while she is visiting the family. The special adventures are then recorded in the journal and read to the class at Monday's group. One adventure was told through magazine pictures with a few gestures of sign language to interpret. Brittney and her mom had washed Sally Rose in the washing machine and they told about the experience from Sally Rose's

Sally Rose goes home in a special bag with a journal. She travels with a different child each weekend and her adventures are recorded by the family and shared at group time on Monday morning.

point of view. The children were intrigued and amused. In other adventures Sally Rose was carried off by the family dog, left at McDonald's all night, and went shopping for some new pajamas.

Newsletter.   Each week a brief newsletter goes home with a synopsis of the week and any story-related events. Attached to this letter is a complete version of the story for the upcoming week. This is particularly helpful for families who don't own the book or have access to a library. It also gives parents a chance to see the particular version being used in case they would like to share other renditions or discuss the one sent home. Translations into the family's first language or a taped version for nonreaders are options that some settings have incorporated with success.

The newsletter can also include literacy events in the community, such as: upcoming family movies, story hours, puppet shows, plays, university events, museums, zoo, and the circus. These experiences with the family open up wonderful opportunities for children to share their learning during group times and with peers, using artwork, dramatic play, and the like.

Video Creation.   A group of parents gathered one evening in the preschool to produce a videotape of "The Three Billy Goats Gruff" for their children. They dressed up in makeshift costumes, set up their homemade props, and carried on like their kids. There was much self-conscious laughter at first, but after a trial run, the parents became hams! One mother played the narrator and introduced herself as Laura's mother. Everyone followed suit with an introduction such as: "I am Billy's father, but today I am also the Biggest Billy Goat Gruff." It was marvelous fun for the parents that night, but when we showed it to the children the next day, they seemed nonplussed! We think the costumes disguised the parents too well, so that children couldn't tell which one was their parent. It's probably a good idea to make sure costumes do not obscure faces when dealing with very young viewers. If you think the children are ready to comprehend disguises, have parents put on the face paint, mask, and so on in full view of the camera so the children can see the transformation.

Story Retellers.   Many settings have developed a story time "take home kit" to go home on loan with their families. The kit can include anything a setting has available to enhance a family's enjoyment of sharing the story experience. It is important to make the materials as durable and aesthetic as possible and to have "spare parts" available. Losses and breakage are to be anticipated. Some suggestions:

- Commercial tapes with accompanying books
- Teacher, parent, or siblings reading books on tape with the version familiar to the class
- Cover books that accompany tapes with clear contact paper or take books apart and enclose each page in a small plastic bag. Use rings to hold book together.
- Explore garage sales, store closures, end-of-conference/convention sell-outs to gather miniature pieces to use in story retelling kits. Encourage use of what families may have at home—three stuffed bears, or three different size rocks for the bears, a Barbie Doll, and jar lids for bowls. Some settings have enclosed paper, crayons, fur scraps, and materials relevant to the story for puppet or book making.
- Tapes and books could be done in the languages represented in your group. Universities, libraries, and churches often have people who can tap the resources necessary to help with this process.

Nothing encourages families to participate better than the chance to join their children in a story presentation.

- One center videotaped the group acting out *Corduroy Bear* and enclosed that tape and the book for special trips to a different home each night.

The important point is family involvement and shared enjoyment with the literacy experience. In homes in which parents are themselves struggling with literacy, these simple stories help them learn to read with their child. Adding videotapes and audiotapes can be very reinforcing. Parents can become caught up in their child's interest and love of books, motivating them to try reading, perhaps after years of failure with the reading experience.

Other Playful and Meaningful Extensions

Enthusiasm and a sincere enjoyment of the journey are contagious. Here are some ideas developed in various settings that truly enhanced the home/school connection and captivated the children's interest.

Becoming the Character. One day a group of children had just gathered for circle time. Suddenly they heard a rap at the window. The children ran over to the window with their assistant teacher and saw "Wee Willie Winkie" peering through at them in a night shirt, night cap, and candle. (This was really their teacher in costume.) He was invited in and joined circle time. He told them a story about himself as a boy and how he got the job of being the night person in charge of making sure children got to bed on time. He then incorporated *their* bedtime rituals into the story that he had gathered from the families. For example: "Jessie, I watched mom read you *Corduroy Bear* before you went to bed last week and Melinda, I hear you love to feed your dog before you crawl into bed. . . ." This particular teacher likes to bring the children personally into the story time as much as possible.

Storybox. The storybox includes the miniature world pieces for a particular story. An adult or a child can lead. The object is to recall the characters, plot, scene, or action of a story. The leader asks what story is being told this week. Let's say it's "The Three Little Pigs." The children then try to recall what the story involves: pigs, wolf, three types of houses, barrel, apple tree, ladder, or whatever the version being told requires. Each time the children remember a piece, they bring it out and set it up on a table. When all the pieces are out of the box, the top of the box or the table become the stage for retelling the story. It's a nice way to introduce terms such as characters, props, setting the scene, plot, action, and the like.

"Tell Me Another Story, Mom, and Put Me in It!"   Children love to hear stories about their beginnings and early years. Told at bedtime, these stories are particularly soothing and a means of sharing a child's family history.

Our children used to love to hear about the time our dog, Josephine, delivered seven puppies between the kitchen and the backyard. After building a special pen for them in a hallway, Chip, aged three, decided to be Josephine's eighth puppy. He quietly got up *very* early one morning, slipped into their pen, curled up right in the middle of all the puppies, and fell asleep. When Jennifer decided to join him, all "eight" puppies woke up and the wild rumpus started!

Photo Stories.   Photo albums containing selected pictures from the children's own lives with simple memories and short stories are a beautiful introduction or extension to their literacy and emotional experiences. One family expanded the idea by coordinating an audiotape with the album. They told stories to go along with the photos and sang "turn the page now" when it was time to move on to the next episode. Extensions of such an album depend on the children's interests and the wonderful ingenuity of parents. Sharing the ideas will help families who might need encouragement to use simple experiences from their child's unique life as a meaningful literacy adventure.

Songs as Stories.   Songs and music are such a universal form of communication. They seem to encourage a breakdown in the language barrier. Songs are stories set to music and their beat and lilt invite humans to participate in a comforting way. Writing the words out in more than one language and sending home a tape of songs in the various languages would encourage a cultural exchange and sharing. Perhaps parents, children, teacher, friends, or relatives could draw or collect pictures to accompany the words of various songs, especially if the subject matter might be foreign to a particular culture.

As a child, I can remember a French friend of my grandmother telling me a story about an old man organ grinder and his trick monkey. She then sang about the monkey's life in the streets of France, in French. I was fascinated. Though I didn't understand a word of French, I loved the song and understood the gist because she told me "the story" first. Joining in on the refrains of a song is also a way of learning a few key words or tunes whether it be in English or another language.

STORY EXTENSIONS, INTERVENTION, AND INCLUSION

The value of the story as an intervention strategy and a meaningful way to include all children has been woven throughout the book. When one story is explored in depth over time, children with varying abilities and talents have a better chance to process the story sequence and its meaning. The philosophy of the storybook journey is that everyone can play a part if they wish to join in the extension activities. If children cannot move freely, speak, or hear, or if they are learning in a foreign language, we must bring the story to them in such a way that they can participate with meaning. No one ever said that Goldilocks had to walk, talk, hear, or speak English. The catch is to seek help in the classroom to translate the story into the child's first language or sign it for the hearing impaired. Many unique and wonderful stories from other cultures have been translated into English for us to share in the classroom. Many teachers have experimented with reading them aloud in both languages with their children. For less mobile children, the environment needs to be thoughtfully developed so a child who cannot move alone can be wheeled in a wagon, wheel toy, wheelchair, or scooter board to join the action. Communication with story extensions takes many forms if we are open and understand the child's attempts. It means keenly observing each child's behavior and working very closely with the families. A child's endeavors to be understood are critical. Teachers will need time, a sense of humor, the ability to accept and support unusual attempts, and, as adults, the ability to model not perfection, but rather to celebrate each child's will to try!

For children who are able to grasp the story with ease and reenact various parts spontaneously, we want them to enjoy their pursuits at their own level as well as to discover unique and creative ways to help the others feel included. Children have a magnificent ability to be compassionate, naturally accepting, and responsible if those qualities are modeled and held in high regard. Meaningful interaction and communication in an inclusive setting challenges the best in all of us. No magic formula or fail-safe curriculum exists. It takes energy, determination, and the belief that we can all benefit if we're willing to persevere through the difficulties and cherish our diversity.

David Hawkins (1970), a well-known philosopher and advocate of sound early childhood learning, wrote an article entitled "I, Thou, It." The article speaks of the valuable relationship between the teacher ("I") and the child ("Thou"). David believes that the first goal in teaching is to encourage engrossment and engagement in learning: ". . .then the child comes alive for the teacher as well as the teacher for the child. They have a common theme for discussion, they are involved together in the world." He goes on to say that it is important that " . . .there be some third thing which is of interest to the child *and* to the adult, in which they can join in outward projection. Only this creates a possible stable bond of communication, of shared concern" (pp. 45-51).

The article must be read in its entirety to fully appreciate Hawkins' keen ability to articulate the essence of early learning. The point I wanted to borrow from the article was the value of "some third thing" to share that would create a common bond of communication and interaction. The "it" part of the triangular configuration for this discussion would be the story. The story can be one very important part of the school experience. It is interesting and enjoyable to both the children and the adult. It creates a united focus and a possible communication link with the adult. It eventually joins the children interactively with their peers through meaningful story replay. They have a common theme for discussion and reenactment. They can become involved together in their extended story world.

The link to home is vitally important to this process. Children with challenges need extended time to play with ideas and movements connected to the story in a safe "practice" arena. They want to share what they like and hear the familiar repeatedly. Bringing the family into the "I-Thou-It" relationship completes the cycle and reinforces the child's security and joy in replaying the story in some form. One mother of a very challenged little boy said that her son "just came alive" when she read *Caps for Sale* just the way they did in school. He ran to the closet for everyone's hats and motioned for dad, mom, and baby brother to join in. This became a nightly ritual for weeks until they could ease him into another favorite he learned at school.

The storybook becomes a reference point that an adult or peer can share to create a common bond of communication and interaction.

Regardless of language, cultural, social, ability, experience, or familial differences, the enjoyment of living with stories can bring us together in significant ways. Stories themselves can play a prominent role. Their universal appeal joins us through the magic of transforming us to another place. From this storybook world, perhaps we can more comfortably view our lives at a distance and in a different form. Perhaps through the characters and the episodes we become aware of the many fears, joys, feelings, and struggles we share in learning to live together comfortably as caring human beings. Sharing stories not only shows us pathways to literacy, but pathways that connect us to each other.

Your own knowledge of the individual child, his or her developmental stage, and unique set of strengths and weaknesses, braveries and fears, will help you in your task. The guiding principle is to listen and observe carefully, find something you know the child does understand and then explain the current event in those terms.

~Rita M. Warren

Little Passengers on Life's Journey

Using Stories to Ease Transitions and Difficult Experiences

This chapter will

- *Share the concept of closure/good-bye books to document and support children's transitions to a new school or center*
- *Develop the idea of struggle books for individuals or small groups to serve as props in working through difficult experiences*
- *List references that have been helpful for children and families during times of transitions and life struggles*

INDIVIDUALIZED TRANSITION, GOOD-BYE, AND CLOSURE BOOKS

Transitions are a part of life. They involve separation, good-byes, and new beginnings. Children often cannot express in words how these changes feel to them and have only behavior to show us they may be excited, confused, or unsettled. It often reminds me of the conversation between the swallow and the rat in *The Wind in the Willows*:

> "O, we're not off yet, if that's what you mean," replied the first swallow. "We're only making plans and arranging things. Talking it over you know—what route we're taking this year, and where we'll stop and so on. That's half the fun."
>
> "Fun?" said the rat, "now that's what I don't understand. If you've got to leave this pleasant place, and your friends who will miss you, and your snug homes that you've just settled into, why, when the hour strikes I've no doubt you'll go bravely, and face all the trouble and discomfort and change and newness, and make believe that you're not very unhappy. But to want to talk about it, or even *think* about it, till you really need. . . ." (p. 156)

The rat didn't want to talk or even think about the reality of a transition until he *had* to. Many people feel that way, but abrupt and unexpected changes are especially difficult for children and do not allow enough time for adults to help prepare the road ahead with them. Like the swallow, "talking it over" with the tangible help of pictures, photos, words, and familiar experiences is indeed more reassuring to young children.

Both endings and new beginnings involve a separation from the known to the unknown. This chapter will focus on how books can prepare children for saying good-bye to and giving them a sense of closure with a school experience. Even if children look ahead to the change as "fun," the reality is they will have those moments of confusion.

Suggested Elements of an Individualized Closure Book

The closure book is meant to be a treasured object for each child to carry with them at the end of the school experience. It is a written and photographic personal history and documentation of a child's experience in the classroom. It is a way of summarizing the time realistically, with feeling, and with great attention to the child's individual as well as group experiences. It says: *you* have been here, *you* are important, *you've* grown, and you are on your way to a new challenge with strength. Although saying good-bye is hard, you will have so many wonderful experiences to look forward to and we wish you well!

Suggested Beginnings

The beginning of the book can either be started with the child's memory of the first days of school or the teacher's. One teacher chose to do it this way:

- This book is all about _____ and his/her special days at _____.
- Describe the beginning days/weeks with: "It's a big step to start school. Do you remember when you first came you (give examples: hid behind mom, played only at the water table, took the guinea pig for a wagon ride every day, couldn't believe you didn't learn to read the first day). . . ."

Highlights of Group and Individual Child Experiences During the Year

Each classroom has those special moments that make them unique and help to connect each of us in the common experience. Examples follow that were significant to one class:

- *Activities*: the visit of a real goat in the classroom, making "wild thing" masks and beads, stuffing huge clothes for a giant, going to the junkyard for supplies, Hiroko's Japanese meal at the long, low table, and our kimono dress-up.
- *Stories we enjoyed together*: acting out *Red Riding Hood* in the woods, stretching canvas for our own paintings like they did in *The Indian Paintbrush*, playing the three bears in triple decker bunk beds.
- *Friendships*: Recognize the significance of the children's particular fondness and connection with certain people, including friends—both children and adults—teachers, therapists, volunteers, paraprofessionals, janitors, cooks, parents, administrators.
- *Funny, meaningful, and difficult moments*: Do you remember when all the mice escaped? When you brought your baby brother to school to have his bath in the classroom? When the children wouldn't play cars with you, but then you learned new ways to ask them and now they play everything with you?
- *Accomplishments*: recognizing or writing one's name, participating in a group, acting out stories, speaking out clearly, overcoming a fear of gerbils, pumping oneself on a swing, tying one's own shoes, whistling, snapping fingers.

Pages That Can Be Included in All Books

Certain universal pages can go into everyone's book, such as:

- This is how I drew a picture of myself on the last day of school. (Be sure to date it.)
- This is a picture of my family or friends, favorite food, house, and so on.
- I can write my name like this. . . .
- This is what I will remember about my school. . . .
- Here is the size of my hand, foot, thumb, and so forth (trace around each).

Endings

The ending gives us all permission to let go and look toward the next step as a positive future adventure. It is a chance to say "You have grown up this year, and now it is time to move on to a new school, class, teacher, and friends."

- Include a photo of the total class with names of everyone.
- Attach some blank pages for the parents and child to write about the things they'd like to do to get ready for the new school (a form of transition planning).
- Include a self-addressed postcard as some teachers have done so the children can send a note during the summer or at the beginning of their new experience as a way to stay in touch.
- Conclude the last section with a sentence or two about how you will miss them and what you will remember most. Then wish them well and let them know they are really ready for the special times ahead in their new school.

Cover Possibilities

- photo of child

- silhouette of child
- child's drawing of self
- large print of child's name with sticker or stencil letters
- white cut-out letters on dark background
- child's handprint

Who Writes the Book

Books can come together through a number of routes:

- The teacher and staff can write books with additions from the children.
- Children can dictate their memories and the teacher can type them up.
- The teacher and child can look through the collected photographs of each individual and write down any memories the pictures generate.
- Family, teacher, and child can all contribute.

Sharing Closure Books with Children

In the last week(s) of school, a time can be set aside to read books individually to each child. Parents, staff, therapists, and other people significant to the child can help at this time. Children can chat about their book, add memories, and enjoy a moment of special, individual attention.

Small groups can gather as a second step to hear each other's books. This is a particularly meaningful experience to children as it only involves hearing a few stories instead of the whole class at one sitting. It also makes it possible to be close to the readers, see the pages, share the memories, and be heard in a relaxed, cozy atmosphere.

If you have children join their parents during the final conference time at the end of the year, this closure book can be a very positive way of sharing each child's growth and personal experience in the class.

A small group gathers to hear each other's closure books at the end of the year.

GROUP CLOSURE AND GOOD-BYE BOOK

In classrooms with large numbers of children and limited sources of adult assistance, a group good-bye book offers an alternative way to gain closure.

Suggestions for a Group Closure Book

Each child has two pages devoted to him or her. One page holds a photograph of the child and the other page has a personal write-up. The process for creating this book is a group time sharing experience. Each child is highlighted during a group time and other members of the group share what they remember about that child. When it was Amelia's turn, the group said:

> "I'll remember her mother bringing in the baby pigs." (Peter)
> "She let me sit on her story mat." (Leda)
> "We giggle all the time—even when we're not supposed to." (Cody)

Procedure

- Focus the children's attention and enhance the literacy possibilities by writing what each child says on a large piece of paper or on an overhead projector.
- Leave plenty of time to do this activity. Type up what was written about each child onto a page and incorporate it into the class book. Depending on the size of the group and whether enough adults are available to create several smaller groups, this activity can take a week or more. Featuring a few children during each group time keeps it fresh and avoids the tedium of doing too many at one time. Naturally, this is not the only way to gather this information, but it has been found to be a meaningful activity to share as a group. The children tend to spark each others' memories of the special things they want to say about each child.
- Have children share class memories into a compilation of thoughts on field trips, special events, significant incidents, class pets, volunteers, and the like.
- Bind the book simply or into a more elaborate version depending on the time, finances, help, the age of the group, and interest of the children involved. The important element is to present each child in a positive way for a class book of memories.

WHAT IS A STRUGGLE BOOK?

The struggle book presents a way to meaningfully assist young children through a difficult time. Most young children find it hard to verbally express their feelings and tend to communicate a need through their behavior. The struggle book story is written specifically for an individual child. Its message is fourfold:

1. To address a difficulty the child is experiencing ("losing your dog has made it hard for you to go to sleep at night. . . .") or clearly verbalize and illustrate the observed behavior when the dilemma is unknown ("once there was a little girl who came to school looking so, so tired. She only wanted to sit on the teacher's lap and suck her thumb. . . .")
2. To help the child better understand what is happening ("it's sad when we lose something we really love. . . .") or ("sometimes it's hard for this little girl to play with the other children when something is bothering her. . . .")

3. To support the child's feelings ("we all feel upset for awhile when our dog dies. . . ." or "a lap is a good place to be until you can feel more like playing again. . . .")
4. To suggest/model comfortable or alternative ways of coping and moving on when a child has been given the needed time. As we all know, this will vary greatly with each child.

Childhood struggles come from many sources—some come from very understandable places, while others are masked. They include such topics as:

new siblings/sibling rivalry

moving (into new bed, room, house, town)

divorce/separation

physical, social, emotional, cognitive challenges

child care/school beginnings

transitions and good-byes

night terrors

embarrassments (wetting pants)

fears and anxieties

death and loss

illness/injury

hospitalization (of self or others close to child)

issues of diversity: racial, ethnic, religious, gender, varying abilities, socioeconomic

pain

stressful home or school life

friendships/belonging

temperament

expectations (of self and others)

change/new happenings

adoption

abuse and neglect

conflict and teasing

CHARACTERISTICS OF A STRUGGLE BOOK

To struggle is to grow—if you have support and understanding during the unsettling voyage.

Individualization

To know children's struggle is to walk for awhile in their "untied shoes" trying to understand the situation from their point of view. Each child presents a unique way of coping when upset; careful observation for clues requires patience. Questions that might be helpful to ask include:

- What is the perceived difficulty that's unfolding through your observations of the child's behavior?
- What does the child seem to be preoccupied with?
- What is the child's particular ability to comprehend the situation?
- What would be the most meaningful information for this child to have for visualizing, understanding, and coping with struggle(s)?

Simple Wording

For the purpose of clarity and meaning, keep the words and ideas simple enough for young children. The important ingredients are to address the feelings (if possible), to highlight the struggle factor to help the child identify with what is happening in the story, to gain an understanding of the issues. Perhaps a child could be exposed to some possible solution(s), but try not to rush this part of the book. Sometimes it's so helpful to develop solutions *with* the children and write down what they say! It's far more empowering and reassuring if they can collaborate on their own solutions.

Illuminate What Is Happening

The struggle book should paint a mental picture of the struggle for the child. You can do this either by addressing the problem head-on with the individual child (e.g., "once upon a time there was a little girl named Sophie and she heard footsteps in her room every night. . . .") or by using a disguised character in the same situation ("once upon a time there was a little dragon named Sputter and she heard things roaming around in her cave at night. . . .").

Some children respond well to seeing themselves in stories and will become easily engaged. Other children may need the distance of seeing the same or similar problem from another's perspective. The proper technique depends on the child's sensitivity and ability to comprehend as well as the complexity of the situation.

Create a Framework/Script

Sometimes adults know the reasons behind a child's disrupting and stressful behavior. They can use that knowledge to develop the script. When an adult observes the child's struggle, but is not certain of the source, it is best to rely on a description of what is observed for the framework of the story. This simply worded description with photos, illustrations, or magazine pictures can help children focus on what they are doing and how it might be affecting them and others.

Differentiate Between Short- and Long-term Struggles

What may seem trivial to us can be anything but trivial to a child. They can imagine things that are even more frightening than the reality of the situation. It might be a harmless garden snake that is going to attack them or trees waving outside a darkened bedroom that look like scary monsters. These fears are *usually*, but not always, short-lived. Often a teacher can discuss them with the child, and show what they really are, most of the time without a struggle book. Long-term difficulties might be reoccurring night phobias, continuous conflicts at home, loss of a parent, or a troubled sibling. These struggles will not go away in a short time and the child is likely to need some tangible help dealing with them—perhaps on many different levels. The book is one attempt. Knowing when to suggest seeking outside help is so very important!

Viewing Struggles from a Safe Distance

Doris Brett (1988) talks about helping children better cope with their struggles by having the storybook characters model a way of coping with a problem the child is experiencing:

> The child learns by observing and, later in the appropriate situation, imitating the model's actions. The modeling can be a real life demonstration or it can be a scene which is imagined by the child. When the child imagines someone else carrying out the actions successfully, for example, getting into the bath and splashing around happily (without being slurped down the drain), it is called covert modeling. Research has shown that when using storytelling as a covert modeling technique, the more closely the story's setting and imagery coincides with the listener's real life situation, the more likely it is that the message of the story will be absorbed and acted upon. Also, if a heroine achieves success at the end of the story, the child is much more likely to emulate the heroine's actions in real life. (p. 36)

Elicit/Encourage Communication with the Child

When a struggle book closely emulates children's situation, feelings, and behavior, it will encourage them more to express themselves. This expression need not be in words. Sometimes children may choose to express themselves more through play or perhaps by drawing the "illustrations" for the story or the emotional issue. One child drew a picture of her family—mother, father, brother, and herself with their arms all entwined—and said: "in *my* pictures I can *make* us all together again—right?" Another child, equally troubled over the separation of her family, drew a picture of her mother, her brothers, and herself on the top of the page with a small picture of her father scrunched in the bottom right corner. She drew a path connecting them and then tore the picture out of the book and threw it away. It provided an opening to share her feelings, but this child was too upset to communicate beyond the act of "throwing" her family away.

The struggle book is thus a sensitive exploration with an individual child that aims to preserve that child's self-image and worth. It demonstrates to the child that someone cares about her and is attempting to understand and share her struggle. Its aim is to help the child come to grips with difficulties or emotions that are making life perplexing. "They don't provide a magic wand to whisk away the trouble and pain of the real world, but they do allow children to learn about themselves and their problems in a way which enables them to feel comforted, supported, strengthened, and understood" (Brett, 1988, p. 60).

Sometimes the book can also help a family look at the situation vicariously or with new eyes from the child's perspective. One mother had no idea that her child was so upset about her going back to work. She had not experienced the regression we were experiencing at school with her child. The mother and the teacher worked on the book together and it was a catharsis for all involved—child, mother, and teacher! Another advantage of having a story is the tangible chance to go back on one's own or with a trusted adult to "digest" the information in the book. It gives the child a chance to master the situation through repeated "readings" at home or in school as the case may be.

For a child who is moving far from a former home and school, the book can be a meaningful transitional object in the midst of turmoil, unrest, confusion, and sadness. Danny had just such an experience. He called us at school to say he was in his new apartment and that Grandma read him the book *lots* of times in the car ride to California. A year later when he called me at home he ended with an announcement that he had lost his struggle book, then found it again, and his mom was keeping it safe for him. It was such a special connection for both of us.

When the child reads the book with an important person in his life, the shared experience can become a treasured memory. It focuses attention on the child. It brings the child and the reader into close contact. If the relationship with the person reading has been troubled, the story can be a powerful means to help rebuild it.

"Sharpie" was a bright, troubled little boy whose abrupt mood swings and violent temper had his classroom on edge (Figure 9–1). Many attempts were made to help him see the consequences of his actions, but for the most part nothing took hold. It was a complex situation and the struggle book that follows was only one way of many that we tried to help this little fellow comprehend. Perhaps "Sharpie's" story will help synthesize this chapter and encourage others to try their hand at writing and snuggling with a child in need of human caring.

EXISTING TRANSITION, GOOD-BYE, AND STRUGGLE BOOKS

A brief list of suggested stories to read to young children during troubling times or as a prelude to anticipated difficulties:

Birth and Siblings
Nobody Asked Me If I Wanted a Baby Sister (Martha Alexander)

I Want to Tell You About My Baby (Roslyn Banish)

Baby, Come Out! (Fran Manushkin)

The New Baby (Cyndy Skeezers)

Look at Me Now! (Jane W. Watson)

Betsy's Baby Brother (Gunilla Wolde)

Jealousy and Siblings
Jamaica Tag-Along (Juanita Havill)

On Mother's Cap (Ann Scott)

John Brown, Rose and the Midnight Cat (Jenny Wagner)

Sometimes I'm Jealous (Jane W. Watson)

Relationships with Older/Aging People
First One Step, Then Another (Tomie de Paola)

How Does It Feel to Be Old? (Norma Farber)

Wilfrid Gordon McDonald Partridge (Mem Fox)

The Midnight Eaters (Amy Hest)

Grampa, Me, and the Treehouse (Barbara Kirk)

Listen to Me (Barbara Neasi)

A Special Trade (Sally Wittman)

I Know a Lady (Charlotte Zolotow)

Death
The Fall of Freddie the Leaf (Leo Buscaglia)

The Dead Bird (Margaret Wise Brown)

Figure 9–1
Depicting the story of "Sharpie"

Figure 9–1 (continued)

Source: Sue McCord. For copies of *Sharpie*, write to Sue McCord at: University of Colorado, Boulder, Box 409, Department CDSS, Boulder, CO 80409.

Everett Anderson's Good-Bye (Lucille Clifton)

Nana Upstairs and Nana Downstairs (Tomie de Paola)

Talking About Death (Earl Grollman)

When My Mommy Died (Janice Hammond)

Where's Jess? (Joy and Marv Johnson)

Good Bye Rune (Marit Kaldhol)

Lifetimes (Bryan Mellonie)

Annie and the Old One (Miska Miles)

The Saddest Time (Norma Simon)

About Dying (Sara Stein)

Badger's Parting Gifts (Susan Varley)

The Tenth Good Thing About Barney (Judith Viorst)

I'll Always Love You (Hans Wilhelm)

Divorce/Separation

A Friend Can Help (T. Berger)

The Not-So-Wicked Stepmother (Lizi Boyd)

Talking About Divorce (Earl Grollman)

Breakfast with my Father (Ron Roy)

Divorce Is a Grownup Problem (Janet Sinberg)

On Divorce (Sara Stein)

Diversity

Black Is Brown Is Tan (A. Adoff)

Someone Special, Just Like You (T. Brown)

We Are All Alike . . . We Are All Different (Cheltenham Elementary School Kindergartners)

You Don't Need Words (R. Gross)

Why Are People Different? (B. S. Hazen)

Swimmy (L. Lionni)

It's Mine (L. Lionni)

A Button in Her Ear (A. Litchfield)

Hats, Hats, Hats (A. Moss)

Loving (A. Moss)

Katy No-Pockets (E. Payne)

Our Teacher's in a Wheelchair (M. E. Powers)

My Dad Takes Care of Me (P. Quinlan)

Spectacles (E. Raskin)

The Sneetches (Dr. Seuss)

Your Skin and Mine (P. Showers)

About Handicaps (S. B. Stein)

The Tortoise and the Hare (J. Stevens)
My Daddy Is a Nurse (M. Wandro)
A Chair for My Mother (V. Williams)
William's Doll (C. Zolotow)

10

The End Is Just a Beginning

Resources for the Journey

FINAL THOUGHTS

The following collection of children's book titles incorporate the suggestions of many inspiring children, teachers, parents, and two wonderful book stores! They are books that lend themselves well to a journey within classroom settings, in child-care settings, or in the home. The versions of the classics that have been included reflect a more peaceful solution to life's dilemmas. I have done this purposefully because I believe that very young children need not be exposed to the violence in storybooks during the school or center's group time. The media already bombards them with violence, and too many children experience violence in their own lives. Different versions of the classics are encouraged for reading at home, where the family knows the child's understanding and tolerance and can instill the values they would like to foster as a family. With a diverse population in the classroom, my intent is to present a less frightening, more positive portrayal of story events. I sanction much of what Bettelheim wrote in *The Uses of Enchantment* about the message that fairy tales convey to children. That message is that there are difficulties in life that are unavoidable . . . that this is part of being human. We can shy away from life's hardships or steadfastly take them on—maybe even master great obstacles to become victorious in the end. Children need suggestions in symbolic form about how to deal with life's tougher issues. They also need our support during their struggle to gain a deeper understanding of those issues. I believe this is best done in the home with the youngest children, however, not in the large group setting of a classroom. Children's fears may not be apparent while they are with you in a group; night terrors or childlike struggles to understand and cope may rear their ugly heads at home in the middle of the night. If the parents have chosen to read the version of *Red Riding Hood* in which grandma gets eaten by the wolf, they at least have a clue to the possible source of the fear and can begin to help.

By no means are *all* the books we love, prize, or have used in the past included on this list. Hardly a day goes by where a new book suggestion doesn't appear on my desk from a parent, student, colleague, or in the hand of a child. The list is merely a beginning and will grow forever thanks to the sharing network of fellow book lovers!

The adult bibliography includes a very personal selection of resources that have been particularly meaningful to me over the years. If I were to pick my all-time favorite, it would be *The Logic of Action* by Francis Hawkins. She captures the inner spirit of children and shares the essence of what it means to teach through one's own learning about the development of individuals. Frannie shares a marvelous pathway to learning and I've tried to journey in that spirit to the land of literacy.

The end of this journey really is only a beginning. May your backpack be filled with new visions, dreams, and ideas to pursue in your future days with young children. Happy journey ahead!

~Sue McCord

Favorite Stories for the Journey with Young Children

Nursery Rhymes

"Humpty Dumpty"

"Miss Muffet"

"Wee Willie Winkie"

"Mary Had a Little Lamb"

"Jack Horner"

"Jack Be Nimble"

"Jack and Jill"

"Old Mother Hubbard"

"There Was an Old Woman"

"Sing a Song of Sixpence"

"Hickory Dickory Dock"

"Hey Diddle Diddle"

"Mary Mary"

"Old King Cole"

"Little Bo Peep"

"Little Boy Blue"

"One Two Buckle My Shoe"

"Baa Baa Black Sheep"

Suggested Sources

Wright, B. (1944). *The real Mother Goose*. Chicago: Rand McNally & Co.

Weikart, D. (1979). *Young children in action*. Ypsilanti, MI: High/Scope.

Jones, C. (1992). *Hickory, Dickory Dock and other nursery rhymes*. Boston: Houghton Mifflin.

de Angelis, M. (1953). *Book of nursery and Mother Goose rhymes*. New York: Doubleday.

McClosky, P. (1991). *Find the real Mother Goose*. New York: Checkerboard Press.

Larche, D. (1985). *Father Gander nursery rhymes*. Santa Barbara, CA: Advocacy Press.

Hennessy, B. G. (1991). *The missing tarts*. New York: Viking Penguin.

Loomans, D., Kolberg, K., & Loomans, J. (1991). *Positively Mother Goose*. Tiburon, CA: H. J. Kramer.

de Paola, T. (1981). *The comic adventures of Old Mother Hubbard and her dog*. New York: Harcourt Brace Jovanovich.

Poems/Rhymes/Rhythms

Lear, E. (1986). *The owl and the pussycat*. New York: Putnam.

Stevenson, R. L. *My Shadow*.

Five little pumpkins. (Author unknown).

Galdone, P. (1986). *Three little kittens*. New York: Clarion/Houghton Mifflin.

Milne, A. A. (1986). *Now we are six*. New York: Dell.

Sendak, M. (1962). *Chicken soup with rice*. New York: Harper & Row.

McCord, D. (1980). *Everytime I climb a tree*. Boston: Little, Brown.

O'Neill, M. (1961). *Hailstones and halibut bones*. New York: Doubleday.

Silverstein, S. (1974). *Where the sidewalks end*. New York: Harper & Row.

Fleischman, P. (1988). *Joyful noise*. New York: Trumpet Club.

Martin, B. (1989). *Chicka chicka boom! boom!* New York: Simon & Schuster.

Milne, A. A. (1927). *Now we are six*. New York: Dell.

Hoberman, M. A. (1978). *A house is a house for me*. New York: Viking Press.

Hague, M. (1989). *Bear hugs*. New York: Henry Holt.

Gag, W. (1928). *Millions of cats*. New York: Putnam.

Prelutsky, J. (1986). *Read-aloud rhymes for the very young*. New York: Knopf.

Schenk de Regniers, B. (Ed.). (1988). *Sing a song of popcorn: Every child's book of poems*. New York: Scholastic.

There once was a turtle. (Author unknown).

Dr. Seuss. (1960). *Green eggs and ham*. New York: Random House.

Carlstrom, N. W. (1986). *Jesse Bear, what will you wear?* New York: Macmillan.

Rosen, M. (1989). *We're going on a bear hunt*. New York: Margaret McElderry Books.

Mosel, A. (1986). *Tikki tikki tembo*. New York: Scholastic.

Wood, A. (1984). *The napping house*. San Diego: Harcourt Brace Jovanovich.

Sendak, M. (1970). *In the night kitchen*. New York: Puffin.

Grossman, V., & Long, S. (1991). *Ten little rabbits*. San Francisco: Chronicle.

Fairy bubble. (Author unknown).

Songs

Frosty the snowman. (1973). Golden Books/Golden Press. Racine, WI: Western Publishing.

Scott, L. B., & Pavelko, V. (1988). *Five little speckled frogs*. Salem, OR: Nellie Edge, 1988.

Spier, P. (1961). *The fox went out*. New York: Doubleday.

Lipton, L., & Yarrow, P. *Puff the magic dragon*. From "Peter, Paul and Mommy". Warner Bros., Seven Arts Records.

Westcott, N. (1980). *There was an old lady who swallowed a fly*. Boston: Little, Brown.

Silverstein, S. (1974). Boa constrictor. From *Where the sidewalk ends*. New York: Harper & Row.

Hole in the bottom of the sea. (Author unknown).

Aliki. (1974). *Go tell Aunt Rhody*. New York: Macmillan.

Wadsworth, O. A. (1971). *Over in the meadow*. New York: Scholastic.

Adams, P. (1979). *There were ten in the bed*. Chicago: Child's Play Press.

Langstaff, J. (1974). *A-hunting we will go*. New York: Margaret McElderry Books.

Little white duck. (Author unknown).

Aliki. (1981). *Hush little baby*. Englewood Cliffs, NJ: Prentice-Hall.

Zelinsky, P. (1990). *Wheels on the bus*. New York: Dutton.

Shannon, G. (1981). *Lizard's song*. New York: Mulberry.

Palmer, H. (1972). *Getting to know myself*. New York: Activity Records.

Palmer, H. (1974). *Sammy*. From "All by myself." Activity Records.

Quackenbush, R. *She'll be coming around the mountain*. Philadelphia: Lippincott, 1974.

Christelow, E. (1989). *Five little monkeys jumping on the bed*. New York: Clarion.

Pearson, T. C. (1984). *Old McDonald had a farm*. New York: Dial.

Westcott, N. B. (1987). *Down by the bay*. New York: Crown.

Kennedy, J. (1983). *Teddy bear's picnic*. San Diego: Tiger Press.

Messenger, J. (1987). *Twinkle, twinkle little star*. New York: Macmillan.

Raffi. (1983). *Baby beluga*. Ontario, Canada: Homeland/Troubadour.

Peek, M. (1981). *Roll over*. New York: Clarion.

Jones, C. (1990). *This old man*. Boston: Houghton Mifflin.

Peek, M. (1985). *Mary wore her red dress*. New York: Clarion.

McNally, D. (1991). *In a cabin in a wood*. New York: Cobblehill.

Westcott, N. B. (1987). *There's a hole in the bucket*. New York: Crown.

Stories: Repetition/Sequencing/Simplicity

Dijs, C. (1991). *The three little pigs*. New York: Dell.

Allen, J. (1992). *Who's at the door?* New York: Tambourine Books.

Trivizas, E., & Ozenbury, H. (1993). *The three little wolves and the big bad pig*. New York: Margaret K. McElderry Books.

Stevens, J. (1986). *Goldilocks and the three bears*. New York: Holiday House.

Hellard, S. (1986). *Billy goats gruff*. New York: Putnam.

Stevens, J. (1987). *The three billy goats gruff*. New York: Harcourt Brace Jovanovich.

Appleby, E. (1984). *The three billy goats gruff*. New York: Scholastic.

Galdone, P. (1975). *Little red hen*. New York: Scholastic.

Piper, W. (1975). *The little engine that could*. New York: Platt and Munk.

Galdone, P. (1975). *Gingerbread boy*. New York: Clarion.

Slobodkina, E. (1940). *Caps for sale*. New York: Harper & Row.

Brown, M. W. (1947). *Good night moon*. New York: Harper & Row.

Numeroff, L. J. (1985). *If you give a mouse a cookie*. New York: Harper & Row.

Numeroff, L. J. (1991). *If you give a moose a muffin*. New York: Laura Geringer Books.

Lindbergh, R. (1987). *Midnight farm*. New York: Dial.

Krauss, R. (1945). *The carrot seed*. New York: Harper & Row.

Nichols, B. P. (1983). *Once: A lullaby*. Ontario, Canada: Black Moss.

Asch, F. (1978). *Turtle tale*. New York: Scholastic.

Flack, M. (1932). *Ask Mr. Bear*. New York: Macmillan.

Hyman, T. (1983). *Little Red Riding Hood*. New York: Holiday House.

Mayer, M. (1991). *Little Red Riding Hood*. New York: B. Dalton.

Gag, W. (1928). *Millions of cats*. New York: Putnam.

Carle, E. (1975). *The mixed up chameleon*. New York: Harper & Row.

Kennedy, J. (1992). *The teddy bears' picnic*. New York: Henry Holt.

Hill, E. (1980). *Where's Spot?* New York: Putnam.

Prater, J. (1993). *Once upon a time*. Cambridge, MA: Candlewick.

Lionni, L. (1985). *It's mine!* New York: Knopf.

Morris, A. (1992). *Houses and homes*. New York: Lathrop, Lee and Shepard.

Morris, A. (1992). *Hats, hats, hats*. New York: Lathrop, Lee and Shepard.

Morris, A. (1992). *Bread, bread, bread*. New York: Lathrop, Lee and Shepard.

Brett, J. (1989). *The mitten*. New York: Putnam.

Kessler, E., & Kessler, L. (1976). *What's inside the box?* New York: Dodd, Mead.

Martin, B. (1983). *Brown bear, brown bear*. New York: Henry Holt.

Martin, B., & Carle, E. (1991). *Polar bear, polar bear what do you hear?* New York: Henry Holt.

Zolotow, C. (1977). *Mr. Rabbit and the lovely present*. New York: Harper & Row.

Eastman, P. D. (1981). *Are you my mother?*. New York: Random House.

Rosen, M. (1989). *We're going on a bear hunt*. New York: Margaret McElderry.

Wood, A. (1984). *The napping house*. San Diego: Harcourt Brace Jovanovich.

Sendak, M. (1970). *In the night kitchen*. New York: Puffin.

Peppe, R. (1985). *The house that Jack built*. New York: Delacorte.

Titherington, J. (1986). *Pumpkin, pumpkin*. New York: Mulberry.

Wood, D., & Wood, A. (1989). *The red ripe strawberry and the big hungry bear*. London: Child's Play.

Arnold, T. (1987). *No jumping on the bed*. New York: Dial.

Brown, R. (1981). *A dark dark tale*. New York: Dial.

Turkle, B. (1976). *Deep in the forest*. New York: Dutton.

Westcott, N. B. (1987). *Peanut butter and jelly*. New York: Dutton.

Lawrence, J. (1987). *Henny Penny*. New York: Modern.

Campbell, R. (1983). *Oh, dear*. New York: Four Winds.

Carr, R. (1973). *Be a frog, a bird, or a tree*. New York: Harper & Row.

Kalan, R. (1981). *Jump, frog, jump!* New York: Mulberry.

Payne, E. (1944). *Katy No-Pockets*. Boston: Houghton Mifflin.

Calhoun, M. (1957). *The sweet patootie doll*. New York: William Morrow.

Minarik, E. H. (1957). *Little bear*. New York: Harper & Row.

Lobel, A. (1970). *Frog and toad are friends*. New York: Harper & Row.

Davis, A. V. (1940). *Timothy Turtle*. New York: Harcourt Brace Jovanovich.

Williams, L. (1986). *The little old lady who was not afraid of anything*. New York: Harper Trophy.

Hest, A. (1985). *The midnight eaters*. New York: Macmillan.

Ets, M. H. (1988). *Gilberto and the wind*. New York: Puffin Books.

Miller, . (1964). *Mousekin and the golden house*. New York: Simon & Schuster.

Lionni, L. (1959). *Little Blue and Little Yellow*. New York: Astor.

Carle, E. (1979). *The very hungry caterpillar*. New York: Collins.

Carle, E. (1984). *The very busy spider*. New York: Philomel.

Carle, E. (1990). *The very quiet cricket*. New York: Philomel. 1990.

Lionni, L. (1973). *Swimmy*. New York: Knopf and Pantheon.

Sendak, M. (1963). *Where the wild things are*. New York: Harper & Row.

Winthrop, E. (1988). *Bear and Mrs. Duck*. New York: Holiday House.

Fox, M. (1986). *Hattie and the fox*. New York: Trumpet Club.

Pfister, M. (1992). *The rainbow fish*. New York: North-South.

Rylant, C. (1985). *The relatives came*. New York: Bradbury.

Keats, E. J. (1962). *The snowy day*. New York: Puffin.

McCloskey, R. (1948). *Blueberries for Sal*. New York: Puffin.

Keats, E. J. (1964). *Whistle for Willie*. New York: Viking.

Yolen, J. (1987). *Owl moon*. New York: Philomel.

Briggs, R. (1978). *The snowman*. New York: Random House.

Martin, J., & Charlip, R. (1963). *Jumping beans*. New York: Scholastic.

Lionni, L. (1967). *Frederick*. New York: Pantheon.

Carlson, N. (1988). *I like me*. New York: Viking Kestrel.

Freeman, D. (1968). *Corduroy*. New York: Viking.

Freeman, D. (1978). *A pocket for Corduroy*. New York: Puffin.

Mayer, M. (1968). *There's a nightmare in my closet*. New York: Dial.

Mayer, M. (1987). *There's an alligator under my bed*. New York: Dial.

Fox, M. (1985). *Wilfrid Gordon McDonald Partridge*. New York: Kane/Miller.

Stevens, J. (1984). *Tortoise and the hare*. New York: Holiday House.

Ets, M. E. (1955). *Play with me*. New York: Viking.

Johnson, C. (1955). *Harold and the purple crayon*. New York: Harper & Row.

Mayer, M. (1977). *Just me and my dad*. Chicago: Goldencraft.

Wood, D., & Wood, A. (1985). *King Bidgood's in the bathtub*. New York: Harcourt Brace Jovanovich.

Asch, F. (1985). *Bear shadow*. New York: Simon & Schuster.

Asch, F. (1983). *Moon cake*. New York: Simon & Schuster.

Brown, M. (1976). *Arthur's nose*. New York: Trumpet Club.

Crowe, R. L. (1976). *Clyde Monster*. New York: Dutton.

Asch, F. (1971). *Yellow yellow*. New York: McGraw-Hill.

Martin, B. (1985). *The ghost eye tree*. New York: Henry Holt.

Barrett, J. (1978). *Cloudy with a chance of meatballs*. New York: Macmillan.

de Paola, T. (1978). *Pancakes for breakfast*. New York: Harcourt Brace Jovanovich.

Lobel, A. (1971). *Frog and toad together*. New York: Harper & Row.

Freeman, D. (1964). *Dandelion*. New York: Viking.

de Paola, T. (1973). *Charlie needs a cloak*. Englewood Cliffs, NJ: Prentice-Hall.

Viorst, J. (1972). *Alexander and the terrible, horrible, no good, very bad day*. New York: Atheneum.

Kraus, R. (1971). *Leo the late bloomer*. New York: Simon & Schuster.

Van Allsburt, C. (1988). *Two bad ants*. Boston: Houghton Mifflin.

Lindgren, A. (1961). *The tomten*. New York: Coward McCann.

More Complex Stories (Plot, Length and/or Concepts)

Zelinsky, P. O. (1986). *Rumpelstiltskin*. New York: Dutton.

La Morisse, A. (1956). *Red balloon*. New York: Doubleday.

Brown, M. (1947). *Stone soup*. New York: Scribner's.

Howe, James. (1987). *I wish I were a butterfly*. New York: Gulliver/Harcourt Brace Jovanovich.

Polacco, P. (1992). *Chicken Sunday*. New York: Philomel.

Lord, J. (1972). *The giant jam sandwich*. Boston: Houghton Mifflin.

McCloskey, R. (1952). *One morning in Maine*. New York: Viking.

Lionni, L. (1985). *Frederick's fables*. New York: Pantheon.

Cauley, L. B. (1983). *Jack and the beanstalk*. New York: Putnam.

Dempster, A. (1972). *Pinocchio*. Racine, WI: Golden/Western.

Potter, B. (1902). *The tale of Peter Rabbit*. New York: Frederick Warne.

Rey, M., & Rey, H. (1966). *Curious George goes to the hospital*. Boston: Houghton Mifflin.

Milne, A. A. (1973). *Winnie the Pooh*. Racine, WI: Golden.

Littledale, F. (1980). *Snow White*. New York: Scholastic.

Prokofiev, S. (1982). *Peter and the wolf*. (Translation: Maria Carlson.) New York: Viking.

Val Allsburg, C. (1990). *Just a dream*. Boston: Houghton Mifflin.

Martin, B., & Archambault, J. (1987). *Knots on a counting rope*. New York: Henry Holt.

Young, E. (1989). *Lon Po Po: A Red Riding Hood story from China*. New York: Philomel.

de Paola, T. (1988). *The legend of the Indian paintbrush*. New York: Putnam.

Martin, B., & Archambault, J. (1986). *Barn dance*. New York: Henry Holt.

Marshalle, J. (1977). *Miss Nelson is missing*. Boston: Houghton Mifflin.

Steig, W. (1971). *Amos and Boris*. New York: Puffin.

Peter Pan (Walt Disney version). (1986). New York: Gallery.

Bonsall, C. (1970). *The case of the hungry stranger*. New York: Harper & Row.

Wilhelm, H. (1992). *The Bremen-Town musicians*. New York: Scholastic.

Cosgrove, S. (1984). *The muffin muncher*. Los Angeles: Price/Stern/Sloan.

de Paola, T. (1975). *Strega Nona*. New York: Simon & Schuster.

de Paola, T. (1974). *Watch out for the chicken feet in your soup*. Englewood Cliffs, NJ: Prentice-Hall.

Taylor, H. P. (1993). *Coyote places the stars*. New York: Bradbury.

Grimm Brothers. (1960). *The shoemaker and the elves*. New YorK: Scribner's.

Lobel, A. (1968). *The great blueness*. New York: Harper & Row.

Van Allsburg, C. (1985). *Polar express*. Boston: Houghton Mifflin.

Lionni, L. (1985). *Frederick's fables: A treasury of favorite stories*. New York: Pantheon.

Yashima, T. (1976). *Crow boy*. New York: Puffin.

Zagwyn, D. T. (1990). *Pumpkin blanket*. Berkeley, CA: Celestial Arts.

Steig, W. (1969). *Sylvester and the magic pebble*. New York: Windmill/Simon & Schuster.

Aliki. (1963). *The story of Johnny Appleseed*. Englewood Cliffs, NJ: Prentice-Hall.

Seeger, P. (1986). *Abiyoyo*. New York: Macmillan.

Kellogg, S. (1984). *Paul Bunyan*. New York: Morrow.

Walt Disney Productions. (1937). *Snow White and the Seven Dwarfs*. Racine, WI: Western.

Ungerer, T. (1958). *Crictor*. New York: Scholastic.

Bang, M. (1985). *The paper crane*. New York: Mulberry.

Ehlert, L. (1992). *Moon rope (Un layo a la luna)*. New York: Harcourt Brace Jovanovich.

Pinkwater, D. (1977). *The big orange splot*. New York: Scholastic.

RECOMMENDED RESOURCES FOR THE JOURNEY WITH YOUNG CHILDREN

Ayres, J. (1979). *Sensory integration and the child*. Los Angeles: Western Psychological Services.

> This book clearly explains the vital role our brain plays in organizing sensory information, what happens when the sensory integrative system is dysfunctional, and what therapies are helpful.

Baker, D. (1981). *Functions of folk and fairy tales*. Washington, DC: Association for Childhood Education International.

> A delightfully small book with a big message: Folk and fairy tales provide children with a frame of reference to evaluate reality.

Bergen, D. (1987). *Play as a medium for learning and development: A handbook of theory and practice*. Portsmouth, NH: Heinemann.

> This book integrates the work of educators and researchers as they explain how play relates to the core areas of development, the curriculum, and the environment.

Bettelheim, B. (1977). *The uses of enchantment: The meaning and importance of fairy tales*. New York: Knopf.

> Bettelheim has a definite philosophy about the role of fantasy in the lives of children. Though his philosophy is controversial to many in the early childhood world, this book is an important contribution to a thoughtful analysis of fairy tales.

Brett, D. (1988). *Annie stories: A special kind of storytelling*. New York: Workman.

Doris Brett has written stories that can be read to young children who struggle with issues of fear, anxiety, sadness, and the like. The introduction to each story is written for adults and gives excellent insight and support to parents and teachers.

Butler, A., & Turbill, J. (1984). *Towards a reading-writing classroom*. Portsmouth, NH: Heinemann.

This book emphasizes the theoretical background for integrating the reading-writing curriculum and its practical application in classrooms.

Carson, R. (1956). *The sense of wonder*. New York: Harper & Row.

Not to be missed! Rachel Carson takes us on a very special nature walk with her nephew and we become privileged observers of her deep commitment to both children and the earth. It is also a beautiful insight into how children learn.

Chance, P. (1979). *Learning through play*. Johnson and Johnson Baby Products Company.

This book is the product of a roundtable discussion on play by many leading experts in the fields of education, psychology, medicine, and human development. It addresses topics such as what play behavior is, how play contributes to development, and how we can improve the quality of children's play experiences.

Cohen, D. H., & Stern, V. (1978). *Observing and recording the behavior of young children*. New York: Teachers College Press.

Observation is such a critical ingredient to understanding individual children. This book provides an excellent guide to not only what to observe, but also how to begin to interpret.

Derman-Sparks, L. (1989). *Anti-bias curriculum: Tools for empowering young children*. Washington, DC: National Association for the Education of Young Children.

This book is a "must have" if you are developing a program that seeks to learn about and accept human differences. It puts theory to practice with excellent suggestions on how to thoughtfully develop an antibias program for children and families.

DeVries, R., & Kohlberg, L. (1987). *Constructivist early education: Overview and comparison with other programs*. Washington, DC: National Association for the Education of Young Children.

This is not a book for beginners! (It's an advanced college course!) DeVries and Kohlberg have done a masterful job of researching what the Piagetian approach to educating young children is and is not. Their review of programs is limited to those that are broadly compatible with cognitive-developmental and constructivist

assumptions. The word *constructivist* refers to children's process of reorganizing their knowledge and understanding to move forward in their thinking. This book is a must for those who wish to be challenged and informed.

Dyson, A. (1990). Symbol makers, symbol weavers: How children link play, pictures, and print. In *Young children*. Washington, DC: National Association of Young Children.

This is a wonderful exploration of children's attempts to communicate through their drawings and beginning print. The examples are rich and educational.

Elkind, D. (1986). Formal education and early childhood education: An essential difference. *Phi Delta Kappan Journal*, pp. 631–636.

Elkind has always been a strong advocate for meaningful, appropriate learning experiences for young children. This article is an excellent example of his ability to articulate what adults must be aware of in the education of our youngest children in a society that is too quick to latch on to superficial learning at the expense of real engagement in learning.

Elkind, D. (1987). *Miseducation: Preschoolers at risk*. New York: Knopf.

This book is a masterpiece for understanding and setting into words the meaning and vital importance of developmentally appropriate practices. It also clearly states the risks of "miseducation" and why we need to make educated choices as parents, as teachers, and as administrators!

Elementary Science Study/Education Development Center. (1970). *ESS reader*. Newton, MA: Author.

A compilation of essays, both philosophical and inspirational, about the essentials of educating our children. Duckworth and Hawkins are among the excellent contributors. Although its emphasis appears to be on science, it is really more about developmentally appropriate teaching and learning.

Fraiberg, S. (1959). *The magic years*. New York: Scribner's.

With talent and a keen understanding of child development, Fraiberg educates us on the essential role that early development plays in the life of a child. Excellent resource for parents.

Goetz, E. (1979). Early reading: A developmental approach. *Young Children*, National Association for the Education of Young Children, Washington, D.C., pp. 4–11.

Goodman, K. (1986). *What's whole in whole language*. Portsmouth, NJ: Heinemann.

This book effectively explains the whole language movement and its profound influences on literacy development. It is a wonderful resource suggesting ways to build a whole language program and to share examples of programs already in existence.

Goodman, Y. (1980). *The roots of literacy*. Claremont, CA: Claremont Reading Conference Forty-fourth Yearbook.

Yetta Goodman's theory on the roots of literacy is based on her years of research in the field. In this article she states that oral and written language develops out of the human need to make sense of the world and the desire to communicate and interact with others. She believes that we must stop instructing children in how to read and start expanding on their immersion in reading and writing activities.

Graves, D. H. (1991). *Build a literate classroom*. Portsmouth, NH: Heinemann.

This book is one of a series entitled "The Reading/Writing Teacher's Companion." Graves presents approaches that encourage teachers and children to rethink the use of time to inspire reflective reading and writing practices, and to systematically evaluate progress.

Greenman, J. (1988). *Caring spaces, learning places: Children's environments that work*. Washington, DC: Exchange Press.

If you need an inspirational and practical book on creating environments for young children, this is the resource you want. Settings for infants through five-year-olds are discussed and thoughtfully shared through photos, quotes, and rich narrative.

Gross, R. (1991). *You don't need words!* New York: Scholastic.

Gross presents an inviting resource for both adults and children describing all the ways humans communicate without words. This is particularly meaningful if there are children in your setting who cannot communicate verbally.

Greenspan, S., & Greenspan, N. (1985). *First feelings: Milestones in the emotional development of your baby & child*. New York: Penguin.

The emotional development of young children and its integration and influence with other aspects of the child's life are discussed in detail in language for the lay person.

Greenspan, S., & Lodish, R. (1991). School literacy: The real ABCs. *Phi Delta Kappan*, December 1991, pp. 301-308.

This article thoughtfully develops a case for an approach to education that identifies (through observation) and mobilizes (by how we teach) each child's individual and unique way of attending, relating to others, and communicating. The bottom line is that children need to know *how* to learn.

Halpren, A., & Todd, J. (1983). Beyond programs . . . uncovering the child. *Childhood Education*. May/June, p. 23.

A parent and a teacher team up in this article to reveal how each views the way a child learns and how mentoring and examples change a teaching approach.

Harste, J., Woodward, V., & Burke, C. (1984). *Language stories and literacy lessons*. Portsmouth, NH: Heinemann.

The theoretical perspective in this book examines teaching in relationship to learning, curriculum, and literacy development. The book provides a clear vision of what we as educators need to learn in order to help children reach their full potential as literacy learners.

Hawkins, F. P. (1969). *The logic of action: Young children at work*. New York: Pantheon.

An experienced and dedicated teacher vividly demonstrates the value of play and exploration as vital learning tools for six children with hearing impairments. The children move from passive to active learners and are introduced to enriching, engaging, and fascinating materials.

Healy, J. (1989). *Your child's growing mind*. New York: Doubleday.

A clearly written guide for understanding the growing mind of a child from an experienced teacher who gained her expertise in the classroom working with children and through her extensive research in brain development.

Healy, J. (1990). *Endangered minds*. New York: Simon & Schuster.

Jane Healy clearly explains why our present-day lifestyle sabotages our children's language acquisition, thinking, and personal success. She makes it very clear that parents, schools, and the culture at large have some serious choices to make. She offers priorities and strategies compatible with the nature of childhood and demonstrates how parents and teachers can encourage lifelong learning.

Hereford, N. J., & Schall, J. (1991). *Learning through play: Dramatic play*. New York: Scholastic.

This book is one of a series on learning through play. The other books address art, blocks, science, and language. Each book has an excellent discussion of the theories associated with the topic being addressed and a clearly developed section on activities labeled by age group.

Hohmann, M., Bonet, B., & Weikart, D. (1979). *Young children in action*. Ypsilanti, MI: High/Scope.

What a resource for new teachers as well as a reference for those with more experience! This book develops a framework for what Hohmann and Weikart have labeled developmentally valid education. One of the most helpful aspects of this book is a blocked-off section, "Key Experiences," which simply outlines the significance of each activity and the learning potential. It is a resource packed with ideas that are based on sound early childhood theories of development.

Holdaway, D. (1979). *The foundations of literacy*. New York: Ashton Scholastic.

Don Holdaway refers to his book as a book by a teacher for teachers, "a child-watcher's guide to literacy." With remarkable clarity, Holdaway guides teachers with humor and skill toward an understanding of how they can support children's development of competence in literacy.

Jensen, M. (1985). Story awareness: A critical skill for early reading. *Young Children*, pp. 20–24.

This is a very helpful article that shows how reading stories aloud to young children can substantially contribute to their story knowledge and their awareness of reading. It also discusses how story awareness develops, ways to assess story awareness, and activities to enrich story awareness.

Jersild, A. (1955). *When teachers face themselves*. New York: Teachers College Press.

This is an oldy, but goody. Jersild presents his important theory that to do our best teaching we must first really understand ourselves. In this book he has developed a way for teachers to look at what they are doing and why.

Johnson, D., Johnson, R., & Smith, K. (1991). *Active learning: Cooperation in the college classroom*. Edina, MN: Interaction Book Co.

This is an excellent resource for teachers who would like to embark on cooperative learning in their classrooms and with their colleagues. It presents the theory and gives very helpful ideas on how to develop a spirit of shared learning.

Jones, E. (1978). *Joys and risks in teaching young children*. Pacific Oaks, CA: Pacific Oaks College & Children's School.

There are certainly joys and risk in teaching! Elizabeth Jones shares her expertise using rich stories and examples to help us understand the challenge of risks and the role of joy in our life with young children.

Jones, E. (1986). *Teaching adults: An active learning approach*. Washington, DC: National Association for the Education of Young Children.

This book actually takes us through a course in active learning with adults. It illustrates the impor-
tance of teaching adults the way many believe that children should be taught: *actively* engaging all in the learning process. This is a must for early childhood training and education programs.

Katz, L. (1985). *What should young children be doing?*. Urbana, IL: University of Illinois.

Lilian Katz has spent many years researching and writing about the intellectual and social aspects of education. In this article she discusses curriculum and the methods of teaching that best serve children's long-term development. She also discusses four categories of learning: knowledge, skills, feelings, and dispositions; the risks of early academic instruction; and a variety of teaching methods. It is a brief, excellent article for all teachers.

Lickona, T. (1991). *Educating for character*. New York: Bantam.

In these times when our families and schools are searching for ways to help children develop character, respect, and responsibility, this book provides an excellent guide! If we want to create a humane and decent society, we're going to have to confront the controversial issue of values both at home and in the schools. *Educating for Character* effectively shares programs from across the country that are working toward this goal and develops guidelines for those wishing to establish a program in moral development.

McVitty, W. (Ed.). (1985). *Children and learning*. Rosebery, New South Wales: Bridge Printery.

This book presents stimulating ideas for teachers under three headings: changing views about learning, children and literacy learning, and children learning through media. The underlying philosophy is that we need to shift away from teaching *what* to think toward learning *how* to think!

Milgram, J., & Sciarra, D. (1974). *Childhood revisited*. New York: Macmillan.

Well-known people share memories and stories about their own childhood. Their perceptions of their early years offer very revealing studies in human development.

Miller, K. (1985). *Ages and stages*. Marshfield, MA: Telshare.

This book focuses on the typical development of children from birth through age eight. Each chapter discusses a particular age and stage of development and suggests activities appropriate for that developmental period.

Miller, S. (1991). *Learning through play: Language*. New York: Scholastic.

This is a practical guide for teaching young children with an eye toward a playful approach to enhancing the development of language. There is an excellent, readable blend of theory and activities.

Mitchell, A., & David, J. (1992). *Explorations with children*. Mt. Rainier, MD: Gryphon.

Monighan-Nourot, P., Scales, B., Van Hoorn, J., & Almy, M. (1987). *Looking at children's play: A bridge between theory and practice*. New York: Teachers College Press.

> Drawing on their experience as teachers and on their review of the literature, the authors talk about the value and distinguishing features of play and present guidelines for assessing the meaning of play.

Neugebauer, B. (Ed.). (1992). *Alike and different: Exploring our humanity with children*. Washington, DC: National Association for the Education of Young Children.

> This is an excellent collection of resources from researchers, educators, and parents on the struggle to live in our changing world. It is a guide for helping children and adults to learn more about acceptance, understanding, and the celebration of our differences. A must-have for every school library!

Pearpoint, J., Forest, M., & Snow, J. (1992). *The inclusion papers: Strategies to make in inclusion work*. Toronto: Inclusion Press.

> The basic premise of this collection of articles is that there is a growing recognition of the importance and commitment to educating all of our children in inclusive settings. It addresses the issues, difficulties, and joys of the inclusion process and gives excellent and practical guidance to those who seek to thoughtfully include all children in their home schools.

Raines, S., & Canady, R. (1989). *Story stretchers*. Mt. Rainier, MD: Gryphon.

Raines, S., & Canady, R. (1991). *More story stretchers*. Mt. Rainier, MD: Gryphon.

> These two books are a helpful collection of suggestions on how to extend stories into the curriculum. They are set up according to categories such as families, friendship, science, and nature, and simple activities are outlined under each curriculum area.

Rhodes, L. (1981). I can read: Predictable books as resources for reading and writing activities. *The Reading Teacher, 34*, 511–518.

> Predictable books have a special place in the lives of children. Lyn Rhodes' article is helpful in explaining their role in the reading and writing process as well as the activities to support this development.

Sawyer, W., & Comer, D. (1991). *Growing up with literature*. New York: Delmar.

> These authors argue that literature and education are designed to help people find meaning in life and that a broad exposure to literature is a critical com-

> ponent of child development. This book is a comprehensive guide for adults who seek to learn how to use children's books effectively in early childhood programs. It moves from choosing the best in children's literature to integrating literature into the curriculum. This book has one of the most complete bibliotherapy collections for young children at the end of the chapter entitled "Using Books to Heal."

Schickendang, J. (1986). *More than the ABC's. The early stages of reading and writing*. Washington, DC: National Association for the Education of Young Children.

> This book is a must for teachers and parents. It is a delightful read and explains that reading and writing, like other aspects of development, have a long history that reaches back to infancy. It discusses ways to organize the environment to support literacy learning; the relationship between early experiences with books and successful literacy development in the elementary years; and what the reading and writing process entails.

Segal, M., & Adcock, D. (1981). *Just pretending: Ways to help children grow through imaginative play*. Englewood Cliffs, NJ: Prentice-Hall.

> *Just Pretending* offers parents and teachers a glimpse into the imaginative play world of young children and suggests various ways to enhance the environment to encourage imaginative play. It not only looks at the child's development through play, but also delineates the role of the adult as observer and planner.

Sensory Integration International. (1985). *A parent's guide to understanding sensory integration*. Torrance, CA: Author.

> A very concise, straightforward booklet explaining in simple terms the meaning and importance of sensory integration.

Singer, D., & Revenson, T. (1978). *A Piaget primer: How a child thinks*. New York: Plum/New American.

> Piaget's ideas are complex and often hard to comprehend. This little jewel of a book explains Piagetian theory in understandable terms and develops a practical application of his theory. With delightful examples of how Winnie the Pooh and the Peanuts characters' thought processes are very much like those of a young child, these authors illustrate how the young child views the world.

Smith, F. (1983). *Essays into literacy*. Portsmouth, NH: Heinemann.

> This is a fine collection of Frank Smith's classic papers on education and specifically on his theories and views about becoming not only literate, but intelligent. Smith says: "To teach reading and writ-

ing as if their most important uses were for completing tax returns and job applications is like using a telescope as a doorstop." He believes that reading and writing generate possibilities and ideas for the individual that might otherwise never exist.

Strickland, D., & Morrow, L. (Eds.). (1989). *Emerging literacy: Young children learn to read and write*. Newark, DE: International Reading Association.

The authors have gathered ideas from educators and researchers on how literacy knowledge changes from infancy through the early years in school. The book includes many different and helpful examples of ways to approach and support emerging literacy in classroom settings. Much emphasis is placed on the child's keen observation ability.

Taylor, D., & Strickland, D. (1986). *Family storybook reading*. Portsmouth, NH: Heinemann.

The important link between being read to and acquiring language and literacy skills is supported through vivid examples and the work of researchers in the field. This book is a fine resource for families and educators.

Trelease, J. (1985). *The read-aloud handbook*. New York: Penguin.

This book is extremely helpful for parents and educators who would like a step-by-step plan that encourages children to be lifelong readers. The final chapter has an excellent annotated bibliography categorized by ability.

Ungerleider, D. (1985). *Reading, writing and rage*. Rolling Hills Estates, CA: Jalmar.

The reader is drawn into the painful existence of a young boy with a learning disability and the total failure of the system to meet his needs. It is a poignant example of what happens when one feels worthless and powerless in the learning environment.

Warren, R. (1977). *Caring: Supporting children's growth*. Washington, DC: National Association for the Education of Young Children.

This is a beautiful book that addresses the role adults play when they share the caregiving of a child. It is a book about accepting, valuing, and affirming the existence of each human being. It is a gem to be looked at often to remind us of the very critical role we play in a child's emotional development.

Wichert, S. (1989). *Keeping the peace: Practicing cooperation and conflict resolution with preschoolers*. Philadelphia: New Society.

A lively resource filled with clear examples for all adults working with young children who want to convey peaceful values. It addresses how to teach children the skills of conflict management, empathy, communication, consequences, and negotiation.

Widerstrom, A. (1983). How important is play for handicapped children? *Childhood Education: Journal of the Association for Childhood Education International*, pp. 39–49.

Anne clearly states her views and those of the researchers, that play is essential for *all* children. This article is an excellent resource for inclusive education as children with disabilities need role models to grow in their play and social development.

Zukowski, G., & Dickson, A. (1990). *On the move: A handbook for exploring creative movement with young children*. Carbondale, IL: Southern Illinois University Press.

On the Move is a practical guide for integrating creative movement into the curriculum of young children. It is filled with practical ideas from the experience of two teachers who have the whole child in mind when they plan and create with them. There is also a section on working with children who have disabilities.

Catalogs

Hand in Hand

Route 26 • RR1 • Box 1425
Oxford, Maine 04270-9711
(800) 872-3841

Toys and equipment for children from birth through age five.

The Best Toys, Books, and Videos for Kids

Joanne Oppenheim and Stephanie Oppenheim
Harper Reference, NY (1993)

The title tells it all.

Creative Educational Surplus

9801 Jonies Circle, Suite C
Bloomington, Minnesota 55431
(612) 884-6427

Interesting, inexpensive surplus materials for classrooms, child care providers, therapists.

Educational Activities, Inc.

P.O. Box 87, Dept. PC
Baldwin, New York 11510

Excellent source of activity records for young children.

Hearth Song

156 N. Main Street
Sebastopol, California 95472
(800) 325-2502

Handmade toys, craft items, art supplies, and selected books.

Weston Woods

Weston, Connecticut 06883-1199
(800) 243-5020

Excellent videos on the best in children's literature.

N.A.E.Y.C. (National Association for the Education of Young Children)

1834 Connecticut Ave., NW
Washington, D.C. 20009-5786
(800) 424-2460

NAEYC is committed to the education of young children and will provide services and resources to adults who work and live with young children. Particularly wonderful is the journal (*Young Children*) that they publish six times a year!

The Oryx Press

4041 North Central at Indian School Road
Phoenix, Arizona 85012-3397

An excellent source for books and stories with a multicultural thrust. One excellent book they publish is *Multicultural Folktales: Stories to Tell Young Children* by Judy Sierra and Robert Kominski, 1991.

Inclusion Press

24 Thome Cres.
Toronto, Ontario
Canada M6H 2S5

This resource has a multitude of articles, books, and video tapes for sale and distribution as well as a newsletter entitled *Inclusion News*.

References

Allen, F. H. (1942). *Psychotherapy with children*. New York: Norton.

Ashby, G. (1973). Finding a place in space. In C. Gadell (Ed.), *The changing classroom*. New York: Ballantine.

Asmon, F. (1971). *Patterns for designing children's centers*. New York: Education Facilities Laboratory.

Ayers, A. J. (1972). Nonverbal communication in human social interaction. In R. A. Hinde (Ed.), *Nonverbal communication*. Cambridge, MA: Harvard University.

Ayers, J. (1979). *Sensory integration and the child*. Los Angeles: Western Psychological Services.

Brazelton, T. B. (1984, July 26). Emotions enter child's repertory like clockwork. *New York Times*, p. 10.

Brett, D. (1988). *Annie stories: A special kind of storytelling*. New York: Workman.

Butler, A., & Turbill, J. (1987). *Towards a reading-writing classroom*. Rozell, New South Wales, Australia: Primary English Teaching Association.

Cambourne, B. (1988). *The whole story*. New Zealand: Ashton.

Cohen, D. (1972). *The learning child*. New York: Pantheon.

Cohen, D., & Stern, V. (1978). *Observing and recording the behavior of young children*. New York: Teachers College Press.

Duckworth, E. (1973). The having of wonderful ideas. In M. Scwebel and J. Raph (Eds.), *Piaget in the classroom*. New York: Basic.

Edmiaston, R. (1988). *Characteristics of predictable books*. Boulder: University of Colorado.

Elkind, D. (1987). *Miseducation: Preschoolers at risk*. New York: Knopf.

Gamow, I. (1987). The scientist as a story teller. In M. A. Shea (Ed.), *On teaching*. Boulder: University of Colorado.

Greenman, J. (1988). *Caring spaces, learning places: Children's environments that work*. Redmond, VA: Exchange Press.

Hackney, P. (1988, Winter). Moving wisdom. *In Context*, p. 18.

Harms, T. (1979). Notes from a lecture given at Cornell University, Ithaca, NY.

Hawkins, D. (1970). I, thou, it. In *The ESS reader*. Newton, MA: Elementary Science Study.

Katz, L. (1987). *Dispositions in early education: What should young children be doing?* Eric/EECE Bulletin 18, Urbana-Champaign, IL.

Lowenfeld, V. (1935). *Play in childhood*. London: Publisher unknown.

McCord, D. (1980). *Everytime I climb a tree*. Boston: Little, Brown.

Milgram, J., & Sciarra, D. (1974). *Childhood revisited*. New York: Macmillan.

Olds, A. (1982). Designing play environments for children under three. *Topics in Early Childhood Special Education*, 2(3), 21.

Piaget, J. (1967). *Biology and knowledge*. Chicago: University of Chicago Press.

Progoff, I. (1975). *At a journal workshop*. New York: Dialogue House.

Romhauer, I., & Marion, B. (1946). *Joy of cooking*. Indianapolis: Bobbs-Merrill.

Zeity, P. (1974). School as a learning environment. In *Bank Street approach to follow through*. New York: Bank Street College of Education.

Snow, J. (1992). Giftedness. In *Strategies to make inclusion work*. Toronto: Inclusion Press.

Suransky, V. (1982). *The erosion of childhood*. Chicago: University of Chicago Press.

Warren, R. M. (1977). *Caring: Supporting children's growth*. Washington, DC: National Association for the Education of Young Children.

Williams, C., & Kamii, C. (1986). How do children learn by handling objects? In *Young children*. Washington, DC: National Association for the Education of Young Children.

Wiseman, A. (1973). *Making things*. Boston: Little, Brown.

APPENDIX I

Stories and Poems

The following are stories and poems for reenactment. Some you may not know, and some you may know but have had difficulty finding.

Turtle

There once was a turtle
who lived in a box
He swam in the puddle
and he climbed on the rock

He snapped at a mosquito
He snapped at a flea
He snapped at a minnow
and he snapped at me

He caught the mosquito
He caught the flea
He caught the minnow
But he didn't catch me!

Author Unknown

Five Little Pumpkins

Five little pumpkins
sitting on a gate
The first one said:
"Oh my, it's getting late."
The second one said:
"But I don't care."
The third one said:
"There are witches in the air."
The fourth one said:
"Let's run—run—run!"
The fifth one said:
"I'm having too much fun."
Oooooooooowwww . . . went the wind
out went the light

and the five little pumpkins
ran out of sight.

Author Unknown

The Fairy Bubble

I blew a bubble, twasn't any trouble;
A real soap bubble as big as that.
and right in the middle,
with his wings all a twiddle,
sat an elf with a fiddle and a big pink hat.

Now he wiggled his toes. . . .
and he wrinkled his clothes. . . .
and he twitched his nose,
but he didn't say a thing.
Still he just sort of hung on his bubble and
    swung;
then . . . he stuck out his tongue,
and the bubble went PING. . . .

Author Unknown

My Shadow

I have a little shadow that goes in and out with
    me,
And what can be the use of him is more than I
    can see.
He is very, very like me from the heels up to the
    head;
And I see him jump before me, when I jump into
    my bed.

The funniest thing about him is the way he likes
    to grow—
Not at all like proper children, which is always
    very slow;

For he sometimes shoots up taller like an india-
    rubber ball;
And he sometimes gets so little that there's none
    of him at all.

He hasn't got a notion of how children ought to
    play,
And can only make a fool of me in every sort of
    way.
He stays so close beside me, he's a coward you
    can see;
I'd think shame to stick to nurse as that shadow
    sticks to me!

One morning, very early, before the sun was up,
I rose and found the shining dew on every butter-
    cup;
But my lazy little shadow, like an arrant sleepy-
    head,
Had stayed at home behind me and was fast
    asleep in bed.

Robert Louis Stevenson

There's a Hole

There's a hole in the bottom of the sea
There's a hole in the bottom of the sea
There's a hole . . . there's a hole
There's a hole in the bottom of the sea.

There's a log in the hole in the bottom of the sea
There's a log in the hole in the bottom of the sea
There's a log . . . there's a log
There's a log in the hole in the bottom of the sea.

There's a bump on the log in the hole in the bot-
    tom of the sea. (repeat three times)

There's a frog on the bump on the log in the hole
    in the bottom of the sea. (repeat three times)

There's a wart on the frog on the bump on the log
    in the hole in the bottom of the sea. (repeat
    three times)

There's a hair on the wart on the frog on the
    bump on the log in the hole in the bottom of
    the sea. (repeat three times)

There's a flea on the hair on the wart on the frog
    on the bump on the log in the hole in the bot-
    tom of the sea. (repeat three times)

The Little White Duck (song)

There's a little white duck sitting in the water,
A little white duck doing what he oughter;
He took a bite of a lily pad,
Flapped his wings and he said,

"I'm glad I'm a little white duck sitting in the
    water,"
quack, quack, quack.

There's a little green frog swimming in the water,
A little green frog doing what he oughter;
He jumped right off the lily pad,
that the little duck bit and he said
"I'm glad I'm a little green frog swimming in the
    water,"
glumph, glumph, glumph.

There's a little black bug floating on the water,
A little black bug doing what he oughter,
He tickled the frog on the lily pad
That the little duck bit and he said,
"I'm glad I'm a little black bug floating on the
    water,"
chirp, chirp, chirp.

There's a little red snake lying in the water,
A little red snake doing what he oughter,
He frightened the duck and the frog so bad
He ate the little bug and he said,
"I'm glad I'm a little red snake lying in the water,"
sss, sss, sss.

Now there's nobody left sitting in the water,
Nobody left doing what he oughter,
There's nothing left but the lily pad,
The duck and the frog ran away. It's sad. . . .
That there's nobody left sitting in the water,
boo, hoo, hoo.

The two following poems are variations of a chant
for "The Three Bears." Version one:

Once Upon a Time in a Nursery Rhyme

Once upon a time in a nursery rhyme
There were three bears: A mama bear, a papa
    bear, a little bitty wee bear.
One day they went a walkin' and a talkin' in the
    deeeeeeep woods.
Along came a girl with long flowing golden curls.
Her name was Goldilocks!
She knocked on the door. No one was there.
She didn't care. She walked right in and had her-
    self a ball.
Home came the three bears.
"Who's been eating my porridge?" said that papa
    bear, the papa bear.
"Who's been eating my porridge?" said the mama
    bear, the mama bear.
"Hey mama, wee bear," said the little wee bear.
"Someone has broken my chair!"
Ooooh! (hands up in air, wiggle fingers)

Well, Goldilocks woke up, and beat it out of there!
"Bye bye, bye" said the papa bear, the papa bear.
"Bye bye, bye" said the mama bear, the mama
    bear.
"Hey mama, wee bear," said the little wee bear,
"Someone has broken my chair!"
Oooooh!
Version two:

The Three Bears Chant

Once upon a time in a cabin in the woods
lived the three bears.
The papa bear, the mama bear and
(*pop* finger in mouth) the baby bear.

Goldilocks was walking in the woods one day
She knocked at the door (knock twice on wood)
but no one was there
no no no no one was there.
She walked right in and she made herself at
    home.
She didn't care.
no no no she didn't care.

The three bears came home.
low voice: "Who's been eating my porridge," said
    the papa bear.
higher voice: "Who's been eating my porridge,"
    said the mama bear.
Say hey ba ba ree bear—said the little wee bear
"Someone has eaten mine up—wah" (rub eyes).

"Who's been sitting in my chair," said the papa
    bear.
"Who's been sitting in my chair," said the mama
    bear.
Say hey ba ba ree bear—said the little wee bear
"I think I know who it is!"

Goldilocks woke up, broke up the party
and beat it out of there.

The Little Red House with No Doors and No Windows

There was once upon a time a little boy who was
tired of all his toys and tired of all his picture
books and tired of all his play.

"What shall I do?" he asked his mother. And
his mother, who always knew beautiful things for
little boys to do, said:

"You shall go on a journey and fine a little red
house with no doors and no windows and a star
inside."

The little boy's eyes grew big with wonder.
"Which way shall I go?" he asked, "to find a little
red house with no doors and no windows and a
star inside?"

"Down the lane and past the farmer's house and
over the hill," said is mother. "Come back as soon
as you can and tell me all about your journey."

So the little boy put on his cap and his jacket
and started out.

He had not walked very far down the lane
when he came to a merry little girl dancing along
in the sunshine. Her cheeks were like pink blossom petals and she was singing like a robin.

"Do you know where I shall find a little red
house with no doors and no windows and a star
inside?" the little boy asked her.

The little girl laughed. "Ask my father, the
farmer," she said. "Perhaps he knows."

So the little boy went on until he came to a
great brown barn where the farmer kept barrels
of fat potatoes and baskets of yellow squashes and
golden pumpkins. The farmer himself stood in
the doorway looking out over the green pastures
and yellow grain fields.

"Do you know where I shall find a little red
house with no doors and no windows and a star
inside?" asked the little boy of the farmer.

The farmer laughed, too. "I've lived a great
many years and I never saw one," he chuckled;
"but ask Granny who lives at the foot of the hill.
She knows how to make molasses taffy and popcorn
balls and red mittens. Perhaps she can direct you."

So the little boy went on farther still, until he
came to the Granny sitting in her pretty garden
of herbs and marigolds. She was as wrinkled as a
walnut and as smiling as the sunshine.

"Please, dear Granny," said the little boy,
"Where shall I find a little red house with no
doors and no windows and a star inside?"

The Granny was knitting a red mitten and
when she heard the little boy's question she
laughed so cheerily that the wool ball rolled out of
her lap and down to the little pebbly path.

"I should like to find that little house myself,"
she chuckled. "It would be warm when the frosty
nights come and the starlight would be prettier
than a candle. But ask the wind who blows about
so much and listens at all the chimneys. Perhaps
the wind can direct you."

So the little boy took off his cap politely to the
Granny and went on up the hill rather sorrow-
fully. He wondered if his mother, who usually
knew almost everything that was to be known,
had perhaps made a mistake.

The wind was coming down the hill as the little
boy climbed up. As they met, the wind turned

about and went along singing, beside the little boy. It whistled in his ear and pushed him and dropped a pretty leaf into his hands.

"Oh Wind," asked the little boy, after they had gone along together quite a way, "Can you help me to find a little red house with no doors and no windows and a star inside?"

The wind cannot speak in our words, but it went singing ahead of the little boy until it came to an orchard. There it climbed up in an apple tree and shook the branches. When the little boy caught up, there, at his feet, lay a great rosy apple.

The little boy picked up the apple. It was as much as his two hands could hold. It was as red as the sun had been able to paint it, and the thick brown stem stood up as straight as a chimney. But it had no doors and no windows. "Was there a star inside?"

"I wonder," thought the little boy. He took his jackknife from his pocket, cut the apple through the center. Oh, how wonderful! There, inside the apple, lay a star holding brown seeds.

So the little boy called to the wind, "Thank you," and the wind whistled back, "You're welcome."

Then the little boy ran home to his mother and gave her the apple.

"It is too wonderful to eat without looking at the star, isn't it?" he asked.

"Yes, indeed," answered his mother.

Caroline Sherwin Bailey

The Doubtful Pumpkin Seed

Once upon a time there was a farmer who planted a big pumpkin patch. He placed each seed very carefully into the ground and then hoped the rain and sun would do their job.

The farmer didn't know it but one of the seeds was very doubtful! He just *could not* see how a little flat white seed could ever be a pumpkin. The seed lay buried under the ground for a long while and nothing happened. One day . . .

[Refrain]
The rain came down
and the sun came up

The rain came down
and the sun came up

The doubtful pumpkin seed felt something happening . . . a little *sprout* was coming out of his head. *Oh Dear*, he thought . . . I was right. I'm not a pumpkin, I'm a sprout!

[Refrain]

Soon the sprout began to grow and grow and grow. It grew so long and crawled along the ground that it is now called a *vine*. *Oh Dear*, he thought . . . I was right. I'm *not* a pumpkin, I'm just vine!

[Refrain]

Now the vine was beginning to grow big green *leaves* that spread out across the pumpkin patch. *Oh Dear*, he thought . . . I was right. I'm *not* a pumpkin, I'm just a bunch of big green leaves.

[Refrain]

One day some beautiful trumpet-shaped *flowers* began to grow beside the leaves. *Oh No*, the doubtful pumpkin seed thought . . . I'm surely not a pumpkin, I'm lots of golden yellow flowers!

[Refrain]

It wasn't long before the flowers fell off and little *green balls* appeared in their place. *Uh-Oh*: something's wrong. Pumpkin's aren't little green balls—so I'm not a pumpkin. I guess I'm little green balls!

[Refrain]

Well, guess what? Those little green balls grew bigger and bigger. Then they started to turn greenishly, yellowey, orange. They grew bigger and bigger and bigger and more orange each day until they became—*PUMPKINS*!!

[Refrain]

Wow—I sure was doubtful . . . but now I am one of the very special, happy pumpkins in the pumpkin patch. Maybe I'll be the one you pick to bring to your house (or school). I sure hope so . . . don't you?

Author Unknown
Adapted by Sue McCord

I'd like to end with this poem because it says to me: Let's escape together! Sometimes the world's pace seems all too crazy and I don't always have the brains or the courage to figure it out . . . so let's join our hands and skip down the yellow brick road to the magical world of a good story.

Notes from a Teacher

Perhaps if you knew
that I, like you,
have been caught up
in the whirling funnel
of our time. . . .
that I, also, sometimes
run away. . . .
that we are together here
in the forest somewhere
between the land
of the little Munchkins
and the emerald city of Oz. . . .
(you see, I am
a little bit scarecrow,
partially tin man,
too much cowardly lion)
and I was thinking,
if you'd let me,
perhaps we could go
together
down the yellow brick road. . . .

                    Clovita Rice

APPENDIX II

Letters to Parents

THE JOURNEY JOURNAL
A Family-School Partnership with Literacy

September 2, 1994

It was such fun to see all of the families together at our orientation picnic. We're off to a good start!

We had mentioned our emphasis on literacy at the picnic last night and the development of our curriculum called The Storybook Journey. Each month we will "publish" a few editions of the Journey Journal to keep you informed about how the Journey unfolds at school and to invite the building of meaningful literacy bridges between home and the classroom.

The Storybook Journey emphasizes the significance of and shares the delight in using storybooks as a means of entering the child's world. It explores the important relationship between play and child development; the use of stories to foster human relationships and the inclusion of all children; the facilitation of interesting ways to link the child's home and school adventures with literacy learning; and the creation of meaningful environments, curriculum, and materials derived from the themes and concepts presented in the classics of children's literature.

Each week we select one story to share with the children in depth. The story is told through puppets, miniature worlds, flannel boards, dramatic replay, and the like. These stories are selected by the staff, the children, and suggestions from parents, siblings, and librarians. Hundreds of other books are available to the children all the time and are read to them in small groups or individually. The story we journey with all week is the story that is emphasized and developed fully with the whole group.

The bibliography of stories we've used in the past is attached. Please let us know which book your child is interested in having read to them and any other books you have read that aren't listed. The textbook entitled The Storybook Journey: Pathways to Literacy Through Story and Play is on the table next to the sign-in sheet. Please feel free to check it out for a deeper understanding of the philosophy and implementation of the Journey.

THE JOURNEY JOURNAL

A Family-School Partnership with Literacy

October 10, 1994

We've had a wonderful week with a number of parents being able to share their time with us to help make our Corduroy Bears. Jeremiah's mother, Ruth, and Sarah's mother, Amy, brought in their sewing machines and all Tuesday morning helped one child at a time use the machine to stitch up their bears. John's uncle, Ralph, showed us slides of the bears he photographed in Alaska. You could have heard a pin drop. The interest was so intense. Thank you for the special contributions Ruth, Amy, and Ralph!

This story has seemed to touch the children significantly and we'd like to encourage you to continue to extend Corduroy Bear's "life" at home. Parent volunteers and the staff have developed some take-out packages for you to sign out if you're interested. The following is a list of what is available:

Packages #1 & #2 (two sets)   The book and tape of Corduroy Bear in Spanish and one copy in English.

Packages #3 & #4 (two sets)   Suggestions for making beds for Corduroy out of trash-to-treasure supplies at home (e.g., tissue boxes, shoe boxes, material scraps for sleeping bags, and the like. Package includes a few items to get you started: material, sewing kit, glue, crayons, and wallpaper scraps.

Package #5 (two sets)   Miniature worlds have been gathered to retell the story. Take note of how these were made because you and the children could make others like this for the stories in which your child is taking a particular interest.

THE JOURNEY JOURNAL
A Family-School Partnership with Literacy

STORYBOOK JOURNEY

November 1, 1994

The holidays are coming and we'd like to offer a workshop to all parents who might be interested in creating homemade literacy gifts for their children. The workshop will take place:

When: Wednesday evening, November 10, 7:00–9:00 (child care available; please sign up)
Where: Preschool classroom
Why: Loving books and learning from them is a continuous process; what better gift can we give our children?

Other thoughts:

1. We will also have directions, samples, and materials available all week in the parent room if you'd like to pick them up and make them at home. Abbey, Pat, and Martha will be on hand Monday and Wednesday from 9:00-11:00 if you'd like help on any of the projects.
2. The samples and directions included in the workshops are:
   · flannel board patterns for "Three Bears", "Three Billy Goats", Corduroy, "Red Riding Hood", "Jack and the Beanstalk", Caps for Sale, and "Over in the Meadow"
   · writing and cooking carrels
   · book making
   · miniature worlds
   · puppets, puppet stages
   · story mats
   · book storage packets
   · painting "box easels" and pallets
   · dramatic replay kits
   · dramatic play screen
3. We need the following supplies . . . please help us gather:
   · cardboard boxes (about 2' × 2')
   · copy-paper boxes
   · material scraps (big and small)
   · buttons
   · wood scraps
   · nails
   · flannel
   · iron-on tape
   · pellon
   · cardboard (e.g., back of writing pads)
   · socks, mittens
   · old white sheets (lots!)
   · new sponges
   · film containers
   · dress-up clothes
   · felt
   · elastic
4. Please bring your own scissors, sewing supplies, saws, hammers, and staple gun (if you have them) and let's have fun together.

THE JOURNEY JOURNAL
A Family-School Partnership with Literacy

February 15, 1995

The children have done a wonderful job of telling stories on audio tape. Each one either told about a favorite book or made up a story of their own. We have stories about dogs wearing T-shirts, the Five Marvelous Pretzels, stories in Spanish, a translated story from sign language, and a story none of us understand but it makes all of us laugh together. Do come and listen or borrow the tape so the whole family can hear what storytellers we've become.

Last night in our staff meeting we came up with an idea we'd love to share with you. The staff developed a tape for the children with stories about our own childhood memories and the children just loved it. We'd like to suggest that we develop a tape of each parent telling one story about a childhood memory you'd like to share and one photo of you when you were a child to put in a book to go with the tape.

We have not worked out the logistics, but will do that gladly if you are willing to share a story. There is a sign up sheet at the check-in table, so let us know who is interested . . . of course, we hope that's everyone.

THE JOURNEY JOURNAL

A Family-School Partnership with Literacy

March 5, 1995

We'd like to extend an invitation to all families to come to a special evening at the downtown public library. Mrs. Fox, the children's librarian, has collaborated with us to build on the children's interest in stories about the night. To make it even more fun, she has suggested that the children come in their pajamas, if they'd like to, and bring their families and their favorite stuffed animals to hear the stories too. She will share two of her favorite nighttime tales . . . one of the tales involves a flashlight tour of the different parts of the children's section of the library. This promises to be a delightful experience.

Mrs. Fox said she will also be available fifteen minutes before our story time and afterwards to give out library cards for any family that is interested. Do come!

When: Tuesday, March 16, 1994
Where: Public Library, Downtown Branch (directions attached)
Time: 6:45–7:30

A library card when valued by the family will be valued by the child. It's like a rite of passage and it's such a special privilege to own one. Let's celebrate this experience together and read, read, read with our children. We've enclosed two excellent pamphlets with this Journal to emphasize the importance of this period in your child's life in terms of building a solid foundation in literacy. Reading to your child for only fifteen minutes a day may be one of the greatest lifelong gifts you could ever share with your child.

THE JOURNEY JOURNAL

A Family-School Partnership with Literacy

May 5, 1995

Can you believe that we're only three weeks away from the last day of preschool? It's been a very special year for so many reasons, but the greatest privilege for us as a staff has been the quality of our family's participation in the Storybook Journey process. We can see the profound effect it has had on the literacy development of all the children and that is a joy to behold!

To celebrate the children's transition from preschool to their next group experience, we'd like to carry the Storybook idea right to the end. We're going to adapt "The Three Billy Goats Gruff" theme and have the children "cross the bridge" to go on to their next school. The teachers will be the trolls and ask them: "Who's that crossing over our bridge to go on to kindergarten?" They will each receive a treasured reminder of their year in this class when they get safely to the other side of the bridge. What they eat when they cross "to greener pastures" will be a surprise from the parent committee . . . it won't be grass, but it will be a delicious celebration.

We are going to need some warm buddies to help the children create their outfits for this special occasion. It will be messy so please dress accordingly. If you can lend a hand, let Sue know what days will work best for you. Thank you, thank you, thank you!

Name and Title Index

Subject Index